C0-ASQ-643

WORLD CHAMPIONS
DETROIT TIGERS
1984

"It wouldn't have been the dream journey that it was for "3" without you. I'll always be grateful that I played in the era that I did – and in the city where I did."

Alan Trammel and Christopher Ilitch, President and CEO, Ilitch Holdings, Inc. Chairman and CEO, Detroit Tigers.

3

THREE

a salute to

ALAN
TRAMMELL

DETROIT TIGERS

CONGRATULATIONS, ALAN TRAMMELL

Truly great baseball men are those who excel on the field and have the
character off it to match. There are few in the history of this sport who have
found that equilibrium better than Alan Trammell. We could not dream of
a better representative of the Olde English 'D'.

Tram not only was one of the best Tigers shortstops of all-time, but also
one of the best in baseball history – as evidenced by his induction to the
National Baseball Hall of Fame as a member of the Class of 2018. His
plaque is spot-on when describing him as a catalyst of the 1984 World
Series Champions, and that his profile as a player was well ahead of his
time. Tram hit .300-or-better in seven seasons, while also finding significant
power later in his career. Combine that with stellar defense at a premier
position, and you have a well-rounded player who was able to lead the
franchise for two decades.

We're all so proud that Tram's #3 will forever be cemented on the left-center
field wall at Comerica Park with other legends of the game. He's one of the
best ever to wear a baseball uniform, and we're proud to call him a Tiger.

3

THREE

a salute to

ALAN
TRAMMELL

AL KALINE

I COULDN'T BE HAPPIER FOR ALAN TRAMMELL.

He was a great Tiger - and still is. He's been a great person – and still is.

And now he's getting all the credit that he deserves.

I remember attending his initial press conference after he was elected into the Hall of Fame. I couldn't stop smiling. It was, indeed, an honor that he signed his first baseball "Alan Trammell – HoF" for me.

Tram has long been one of my favorites. I've made no secret of that. As they say, he played the game "the right way" – everything being for the good of the team.

He was scrawny when I first met him, but over the years he matured into a balanced ballplayer combining offense with defense.

Not only that, he was a team leader – never feeling the need to bring attention to himself.

It's exciting – and fitting - that the Tigers have retired his number. I applaud the addition of "3" to the wall at Comerica Park.

Your place in history, my friend, is now secure. I hope you will be a Tiger for life.

3

THREE

a salute to

ALAN
TRAMMELL

ALAN TRAMMELL

THANK YOU, FANS. I MEAN THAT FROM THE BOTTOM OF MY HEART.

As I said at my induction ceremony at the National Baseball Hall of Fame,
"this day is as much about you as it is about me".

And so it is with this book.

It wouldn't have been the dream journey that it was for "3" without you.
I'll always be grateful that I played in the era that I did – and in the city
where I did.

Through thick and thin, Detroit Tigers' fans have been the greatest.

Some day it might fully sink in that I've reached the pinnacle of my
profession – becoming a Hall of Famer and having my number retired
by the Tigers.

But I know when that day comes – if, indeed, it does – my message to you
all who have supported me ever since I signed with the Tigers in 1976,
will be the same.

It's been an honor that you were part of the path. My best to you all,

table of contents

3

THREE

a salute to

ALAN
TRAMMELL

AUTHOR: Tom Gage
SOURCES: Detroit Free Press, Detroit News,
SABR BioProject, John Milner

BOOKS: Gage, Tom. The Big 50 Detroit Tigers.
Triumph Books (2017)

Masters, Todd. Trammell - Detroit's Iconic Shortstop.
McFarland & Company Inc., Publishers (2017)

EXECUTIVE EDITOR: Marc Himelstein
EXECUTIVE VICE PRESIDENT, BUSINESS OPERATIONS:
Duane McLean
CFO: Steve Quinn
CONTRIBUTORS: Mike Bayoff, Mikaela Higgins,
Alicia Juillet, Kathryn Lovelace, Marcel Parent,

Top Shelf Media
PUBLISHER: Todd Carter
todd@invenuemobile.com   p. 734.945.3300
ART DIRECTION/DESIGN: Jan Haringa
jan@performanceinc.ca

All Photographs were provided by the Trammell Family,
The Detroit Tigers, Ilitch Holdings Inc. Archives,
Marc Cunningham, Joe Arcure, Christopher Chagnon,
Clifton Boutelle, Douglas Ashley, National Baseball Hall Of Fame,
Kearny High School, Getty Images, Bill Eisner, Sports Illustrated,
Topps, Detroit Free Press, San Diego Union-Tribune.

Every reasonable attempt was made to give proper credit.
If there is an error, please notify publisher and a correction will
be made in subsequent editions.

Copyright 2018 Detroit Tigers
All Rights Reserved. No part of this book may be produced,
stored in a retrieval system or transmitted, in any form by any
means, electronically, mechanically, photocopying, or otherwise,
without the prior written consent from the publisher, the
Detroit Tigers, 2100 Woodward Ave, Detroit, Mi 48201.

Copyright-The Detroit Tigers baseball Club and the Olde English
"D". All rights reserved.

Printed in the United States of America
ISBN 978-0-692-15927-9

chapter one

3
THREE

a salute to
ALAN
TRAMMELL

the great tram

SOME BASEBALL IMAGES
ARE SO INDELIBLY STAMPED
UPON THE PAGES OF YOUR
MIND THAT YOU CAN STILL
EASILY ENVISION THEM –
AND PROBABLY ALWAYS WILL.

Al Kaline's perfect swing, for example – not to mention his graceful retreat to the wall in right while making a difficult catch look routine.

It could have been any wall anywhere, of course, but the threat of the ball banging off the overhang at Tiger Stadium made Kaline's judgment even more impressive. He always seemed to get it right.

The next image that never fades is both visual and audible. It's the sight and sound of Sparky Anderson barking out from the Tigers' dugout to Kirk Gibson that "he don't want to walk you" – referring to Goose Gossage's preference to pitch to Gibson in Game 5 of the 1984 World Series against the San Diego Padres instead of intentionally putting him on base.

Even as Gibson's home run soared toward the upper deck at Tiger Stadium, Sparky's words could be heard like the eternal echo they have become.

"He don't want to walk you. . .he don't want to walk you. . .he don't want to. . ."

Or how about the image of Jack Morris looking like he owned the pitching mound – because he so often did? Overmatched hitters would miss Jack's pitches by prodigious amounts at times.

Just ask Ron Kittle, who futilely waved at the final pitch of Morris' no-hitter against the Chicago White Sox at Comiskey Park in 1984.

"I've seen Ron a few times over the years since that game," Morris

> ❝He overcame all those early doubts about his strength and became a hitter who could hurt you.❞

said. "He says he could not have hit that last pitch with a barn door."

Such wonderfully vivid memories: Kaline, Anderson and Morris, all of them Hall of Famers.

Now turn your wayback machine to the Tigers' infield, where – if you close your eyes and quietly think of yesteryear – you will recall a sight you first saw many years ago, that of a scrawny shortstop who initially didn't look like he would hit a lick.

He wasn't under-fed, but he looked it.

That kid was Alan Trammell, who eventually hit much more than a lick.

"He certainly did," said Tigers' broadcaster Jim Price. "He overcame all those early doubts about his strength and became a hitter who could hurt you."

There was nothing Trammell needed to overcome to master his position, however. From the get-go, he was a textbook shortstop. From the same get-go, he was consistently reliable

Or reliably consistent. Which one was it? Actually, he was both.

"A lot of people have their favorite Alan Trammell memories," said Morris. "Here's mine, but it's nothing fancy. When the ball was hit to him, it was an out. Time after time, plain and simple, you could count on it.

"Tram's technique of getting to the ball was perfect. He'd make all the plays, up the middle, deep in the hole. But for us pitchers, we loved knowing that mistakes on routine plays, like a hard ground ball, would rarely beat us."

“You want people counting on you… What you really wanted was to have every ball hit to you. I was even that way as a kid.”

It's no surprise that another Tigers' pitcher of that era, Dan Petry, agreed with Morris. To this day, both realize they had no better friend than their shortstop.

"That's my candidate, too, for the perfect Tram play," said Petry, "The routine grounder with that easy overhand throwing motion of his, right on the money to first base. It wasn't flashy, but we all considered it a thing of beauty."

Then again, that's why Trammell loved the position he played.

"You want people counting on you," he said. "What you really wanted was to have every ball hit to you. I was even that way as a kid."

Such was the confidence with which the great Tram played his position. But he was too humble to consider himself a star player,

"I don't know that I was great in any one area," he's often said, "but I was good in a lot of them. I guess a lot of 'goods' add up."

Indeed they do. In this case, they added up to the ultimate acknowledgement that Alan Stuart Trammell deserved to be elected to the National Baseball Hall of Fame.

And with that election, he also deserved to have his uniform number (No. 3) retired by the Tigers.

The intention of this book, therefore, is to honor his many accomplishments. Trammell has been a credit to himself, to the Tigers' franchise – indeed to all of baseball.

"This is a moment that's been in the making for a long time," said former Tigers manager Phil Garner, who was managing the Milwaukee Brewers in 1996 when Trammell announced his retirement at Tiger Stadium after his final game as a player.

Garner insisted that his team remain in the visiting dugout after

the game to watch the proceedings and to hear what Trammell had to say.

"I wanted my players to see what class is all about," Garner said. "You don't get to watch many moments like this."

Years later, the privilege of honoring Trammell for who he is, the way he conducts himself and for what he's accomplished has returned.

It could be felt in the overwhelming applause Trammell received for his induction speech at the Hall of Fame – but also in the genuine love shown to him for deserving to have his number retired.

More than a display of appreciation, it is the fans' way of expressing their affection for the Hall of Fame individual Trammell always has been – as well as for the Hall of Fame ballplayer he became.

Then again, just to be called a "ballplayer" has always been enough for Tram.

"That's the thing," said Jim Leyland. "If you look up the definition of ballplayer in the dictionary, you might find his picture. Add to that the fact he's the salt of the earth, and look what you get."

A second-round draft choice by the Tigers in 1976, Trammell emerged from Kearny High School in San Diego with an innate competitive spirit that appealed to scouts, as well as a firm respect for playing the game "the right way."

"I've had some wonderful mentors in my life that I learned a lot from," Trammell said, "my parents, to my high school coach Jack Taylor, to Sparky Anderson in the big leagues. Working hard to attain your goals was what they all taught.

"Tough love, though, was a common theme from my coaches. That's what Sparky and Jack practiced. They were tough, but fair. I believe that was the proper way to do it."

It also helped, however, that as their pupil, Tram was eager to learn. That's why he asked questions, and embraced the answers.

"They taught me that the essentials of the game never change," he said. "Learn them, practice them. Never take a short cut."

Along the way, it helped to find a long-term sidekick.

At the Instructional League in Florida after his rookie league season in 1976, Trammell was introduced to Lou Whitaker, who was being moved from third base to second. Little did anyone know at the time, but it was the beginning of a dynamic duo which became the longest continuous double-play combination in major-league history.

They were so alike in their careers, Trammell and Whitaker, that they finished only four hits apart – Lou at 2,369 to Tram's 2,365.

"That's storybook stuff," said Trammell.

And they cared so much for and about each other that Whitaker's one regret was that after he started the final

" If you look up the definition of ballplayer in the dictionary, you might find his picture. Add to that the fact he's the salt of the earth, and look what you get. "

double-play the two ever pulled off, he said "I wish there'd been one more grounder hit to Tram."

Trammell played one more season than Whitaker – and amazingly enough, after getting their first hit as major-leaguers off the same pitcher (Boston's Reggie Cleveland in 1977), they also closed out their careers with hits off the same pitcher (Milwaukee's Mike Fetters.)

For Lou in 1995, it was a walk-off home run. For Alan in 1996, it was a single to center, the same kind of hit as his first.

"Talk about closure," he said. "I went out the way I came in."

Trammell was an All-Star six times and won four Gold Gloves. For hitting .450 (9-for-20) against the San Diego Padres, his home-town team, he was named the Most Valuable Player of the 1984 World Series.

His imprint on the Series outcome, however, began as quickly as it possibly could.

Following Whitaker's leadoff double in Game 1, Trammell singled him in for the Tigers' first run. He had two hits in the Series opener, two more in Game 2, and was on base four times in Game 3, including a second-inning double that drove in a run.

Continuing to excel, Trammell hit two home runs in Game 4 as the Tigers took what turned out to be a commanding 3-1 lead.

Midway through Game 5, Trammell was within earshot of his friend Tim Flannery – who played for the Padres.

"Hey, Babe Ruth," Flannery called out to him. Trammell smiled. Nobody had ever called him that before.

It was a magical World Series for Trammell from the start, because for the games in San Diego,

He had a "smell" for the game. – Jim Leyland

he was playing in the ballpark (Jack Murphy Stadium) that he used to sneak into as a kid so he could watch major-league baseball.

"But I had never played there," he said. "To be on that field playing in a World Series, isn't that what you dream about as a kid?"

Trammell, however, never lost perspective about who he was as a player or as an individual.

"This is the kind of person Tram is," said Petry. "When people would thank him for signing an autograph, he would respond by thanking them for asking."

As a hitter, Trammell never tried to be something he wasn't, but overcame the stiffest challenges all the same. For instance, he knew he never was going to be known as a power hitter.

Slowly but surely, however, his ability to hit for power developed – to the extent that for an entire year in 1987, he batted cleanup.

"That didn't mean I was suddenly a slugger," he said of that season. "I never thought of myself as having cleanup kind of power. But I did the best I could – and you know what, I did all right."

Better than all right, he hit .343 with 28 home runs and 105 RBI. To many, he should have been named the Most Valuable Player of the American League that year. But in a 16-12 vote, he finished second to Toronto's George Bell,

With his "scrawny" seasons behind him, Trammell eventually became known for surprising power in that it often stunned the pitchers it showed up against – such as Dan Quisenberry of the Kansas City Royals.

Trammell hit the only grand slam Quisenberry ever allowed.

"Just getting the ball in the air off Quiz was an accomplishment," said Darrell Evans. "It seemed to me that all I ever hit off him were ground balls."

"I've had some wonderful mentors in my life that I learned a lot from, from my parents to my high school coach Jack Taylor, to Sparky Anderson in the big leagues. Working hard to attain your goals was what they all taught."

A fine closer, Quisenbery was making the 300th appearance of his career in a game against the Tigers on May 8, 1984 at Kauffman Stadium. In the midst of their amazing 35-5 start that year, which featured a 17-0 stretch on the road, the Tigers were red-hot when they arrived in KC – with no one playing a better combination of defense and offense than Trammell.

In the fourth inning, he turned a would-be bases-loaded single by the Royals' Don Slaught into a spectacular double play. Without it, the Tigers would have been behind by more than 2-1 when Trammell came up to bat with the bases loaded in the seventh.

On the second pitch from Quisenberry, a wily right-hander with a funky delivery, Tram cleared the wall in left with his slam. Quisenberry would appear in another 374 games after allowing that home run, but never gave up another slam.

Giving credit where it was due, however, he said of Trammell's accomplishment, "man, he hit that ball to North Dakota" – and for that reason, he kept Trammell's baseball card taped to his locker after that.

Trammell would go on to hit .340 during the Tigers' 35-5 start. It was during that time, while Tram was putting on a daily multi-dimensional show, that Sparky said of him "he might be the best player in baseball."

He was one of the best, certainly. And it's only right now that he has become a Hall of Famer whose number has been retired by the Tigers.

CONGRATULATIONS, NO. 3. AND FOR ALL YOU EVER DID AS A TIGER... THANK YOU. ●

out the way he came in – with a single to center.

early

years

THREE

a salute to

ALAN
TRAMMELL

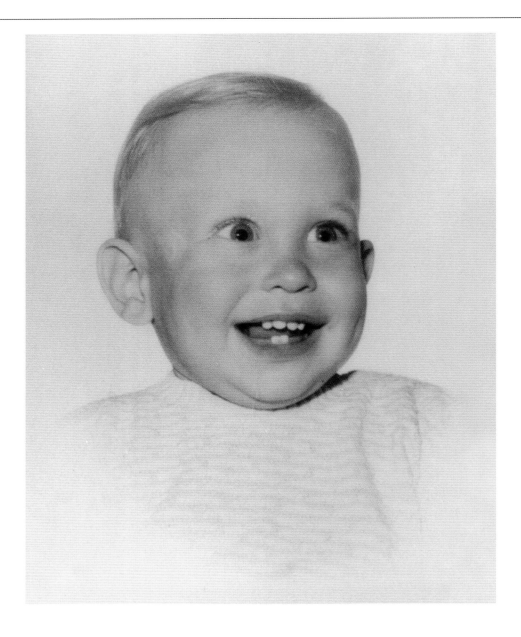

LITTLE BROTHER HAD CLOUT – EVEN IN THE THIRD GRADE.

Nancy Trammell (now Ragsdale), the younger of Alan's two older sisters, reaped the first tangible dividend of her brother's athletic ability.

"When I was in the sixth grade at John Paul Jones elementary school," she said, "we had monthly elections for classroom officers – and for several months I ran unsuccessfully for president. I tried and tried until it finally got embarrassing.

"I'd go up in front of the class to give the campaign speech that my mother helped me with. I mean I tried so hard. And each month I would lose.

"But, finally in the last month of the school year I won."

Where did the votes suddenly come from? Baseball season had something to do with it.

"The boys in the class learned who my brother was," Nancy said. "One of the boys told me so. He pulled me aside and said 'you're Alan's sister, so we voted for you this time.'

Easter and Christmas with his sisters.

"They were three years older than he was – Alan was in the third grade at the time – but he was so athletically precocious that, even with the age difference, the older boys looked up to him."

The Trammell household, when Alan was growing up, was a happy one.

There were his parents, Forrest and Anne; his sisters Lynne and Nancy – four and three years older than their brother – a couple of cats, but only one at a time, a terrier named Adria. . .

And Alan.

"We lived in Santa Ana when he was born," said Lynne, "and moved to San Diego in 1964 when he was six."

Three things pretty much sum up what Alan was like growing up.

"He was always extraordinarily active, running or riding," said Lynne. "He loved his Stingray bicycle. He'd ride it everywhere."

"He was also always smiling," said Nancy.

And he always was engaged in some sort of baseball activity.

"I remember," said Nancy, "that when he played Little League, he could play all the positions. But because he also pitched, he drew a strike zone on the side of our house and was always throwing a ball at it. His focus was on baseball much of the time."

Between meals and homework, that is.

"Spaghetti was one of the family favorites," said Nancy. "But Alan also liked spinach. He hated peas, but he really liked spinach

"Well, that was back when there were Popeye cartoons on television, so we'd sing the Popeye song to him at the table while he was eating spinach.

Telling Santa what he wants for Christmas.

"There we'd be, finishing the song with "I'm strong to the finish 'cuz I eat my spinach" with Alan playing along by flexing his muscles while pretending to be Popeye.

"He was probably only three or four at the time, but he would smile and laugh while we sang."

Tram would also act out his love for all sports with his sisters.

"He'd watch a football game, for instance," said Nancy, "then he would tackle me while shouting 'Deacon Jones!' – Jones, of course being a star defensive lineman for the Los Angeles Rams at the time."

It was all in good fun.

"We'd laugh so hard," she said. "But that was Alan. "

By the time Nancy was 18, though, she could predict with pride what her brother would eventually be doing.

"He never brags about himself, but I love to brag about him. In fact, the day I met my husband as a freshman at UC-San Diego, I told him my brother was going to play major-league baseball.

"Alan was only in the 10th grade at the time, but I was confident about where his talent would take him.

> " They were three years older than he was – Alan was in the third grade at the time – but he was so athletically precocious that, even with the age difference, the older boys looked up to him. "

TRAM'S SISTER NANCY

Tram - eighth from left.

Varsity, Row 1: KY Edgington, Eric Peyton, Tim Beccarelli, Albert Bobadilla.
Row 2: Alan Trammell, David Wimpy, Kevin Baily, Tim Kelly, Bruce
Oliver. Row 3: Coach Taylor, Dave Fitzgerald, Bill Joseph, Bryan
Johnson, Paul Sager, Bart Bass, Chris Turner, David Legg, John
Wenger, Scott Zika, Phil Thompson.

Tram - second row, far left, kneeling.

"Years later, my husband told me he doubted me at the time - like when you say 'yeah, sure' after hearing something you don't believe - but I was right."

In fact, had Nancy said "my brother is going to be a Hall of Famer someday and have his number retired by the Detroit Tigers", she also would have been right.

But that might have been too much bragging at the time.

The two sisters had their hands full trying to keep up with their brother when he was little.

"The truth is, we couldn't," said Lynne. "I remember when we'd go shopping, Alan would run off. He was mischievous in that way. He'd hide under the clothing racks – and was good at it.

"Like at home, he would climb as high as he possibly could on the furniture. Whatever physical

> **❝ I remember that when he played Little League, he could play all the positions. But because he also pitched, he drew a strike zone on the side of our house and was always throwing a ball at it. His focus was on baseball much of the time. ❞**

TRAM'S SISTER NANCY

Tram - third from the right.

challenge occurred to him, he would do.

"Could he get away fast from us? Yes. Could he climb higher than us? Yes. But it was only because he wanted to be active. He never sat idle. He was always doing something."

What Alan didn't do, however, was get into trouble. He wasn't a fighter.

"He was what I would call an ameliorator," said Lynne. "He never provoked physical confrontations. I'm sure he got into it here and there with his friends, but nothing that was memorable."

His sisters never gave him a nickname, but neither did they take away the one that was naturally his.

"When I was in college," said Lynne, "I knew some people who started calling me 'Tram' – and I said 'no, no, no, you can't call me that. That's his name.'"

All these years later, it still is. ●

Boogin' for points is Al Trammel.

> " When I was in college, I knew some people who started calling me 'Tram' – and I said 'no, no, no, you can't call me that. That's his name. "

TRAM'S SISTER LYNNE

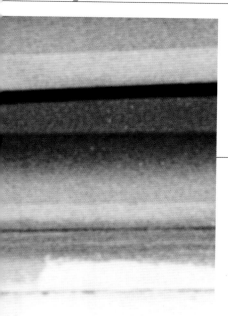

3

THREE

a salute to

ALAN
TRAMMELL

off to the minors

From Bristol to Montgomery in the same year.

HAD IT NOT BEEN FOR GENERAL MANAGER JIM CAMPBELL REFUSING TO PART WITH AN EXTRA $5,000 IN 1976, TRAMMELL MIGHT HAVE HAD STIFFER COMPETITION FROM WITHIN THE TIGERS' ORGANIZATION TO BECOME THE TEAM'S "SHORTSTOP OF THE FUTURE."

That was the year the Tigers drafted Tram in the second round of baseball's amateur draft. Some scouts considered it a reach for them to select him that high – but not Dick Wiencek or Rick Ferrell, both of whom saw a bright future ahead for the slender shortstop from San Diego – in part, they said, because he could hit a curveball.

But five rounds after selecting Trammell, the Tigers chose another skinny infielder from California, a second baseman who would also have a Hall of Fame career – but as a shortstop.

The Tigers drafted Ozzie Smith, who wanted $15,000 from the Tigers to sign instead of the $10,000 they were offering. When the Tigers refused to budge, Smith decided to complete his college education at Cal Poly. He was drafted by the San Diego Padres in the fourth round of the 1977 draft and began his 19-year major-league career in 1978.

No matter, the Tigers had found a star of their own in Trammell. Soon after being drafted by Detroit in the second round of the '76 draft, Tram decided to forego a scholarship at UCLA and accepted the Tigers' $35,000 offer.

"Once I signed, I was committed," he said. "I wasn't going to be stopped. I was going to do whatever it took."

It wasn't long before he was headed to Bristol of the Appalachian League to make his professional debut. Before the end of the 1976 season, Trammell had been promoted to Double A Montgomery, where he hit only .179 in 21 games, but convinced those around him that because of his confidence and defense, he was a candidate to rise rapidly.

"I never managed him in the minors," said Jim Leyland. "I managed Lou (Whitaker in Lakeland), but not the two of them together. Even then, however, when Tram was just a scrawny kid, you could tell from his actions that he had it.

"He could hit a ball to right-center; he could pull a ball. He would lay the bat on the ball without being a Punch and Judy (hitter). And you knew that when he got stronger, he'd be even better, which he was.

"He could hit a ball to right-center; he could pull a ball. He would lay the bat on the ball without being a Punch and Judy (hitter)... not to mention being a great shortstop – one who was out there every day being consistent."
– JIM LEYLAND

"Plus he was a good runner, not a burner, but smart on the bases. Not to mention being a great shortstop – one who was out there every day being consistent."

In 1977 at Montgomery, while getting even better defensively with help from his manager Eddie Brinkman, a former Gold Glove shortstop, Trammell didn't just steer himself in the direction of the majors, he actually got there.

Then again, it was said of Brinkman when he first saw Trammell at short, that he remarked, "my, my, we have something here."

Especially encouraging, in addition to his .291 batting average for Montgomery, were the 19 triples Trammell hit that year, breaking Reggie Jackson's Southern League record. By September, after being named MVP of the league, the 19-year-old shortstop was playing for the Tigers.

By making such a jump, he never played a game at Triple A. ●

Every ballplayer remembers his first contract.

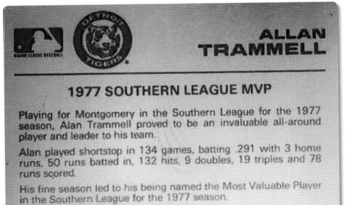

> **ALLAN TRAMMELL**
>
> **1977 SOUTHERN LEAGUE MVP**
>
> Playing for Montgomery in the Southern League for the 1977 season, Alan Trammell proved to be an invaluable all-around player and leader to his team.
>
> Alan played shortstop in 134 games, batting .291 with 3 home runs, 50 runs batted in, 132 hits, 9 doubles, 19 triples and 78 runs scored.
>
> His fine season led to his being named the Most Valuable Player in the Southern League for the 1977 season.
>
> © 1990 THE STAR CO.   1 of 2,000 SETS   51

" Once I signed, I was committed. I wasn't going to be stopped. I was going to do whatever it took. **"**

Rock star or ballplayer?

chapter four

HELLO, tigers

3

THREE

a salute to

ALAN
TRAMMELL

Drafted in '76, Tiger in '77.

H E KNEW HE LOOKED YOUNG BECAUSE HE WAS YOUNG. BUT ALAN TRAMMELL DIDN'T WANT ANYONE THINKING HE WAS TOO YOUNG.

So when a reporter asked him how old he was on the day he was called up to the majors, Trammell replied "19. . .and a half."

From the time he was drafted in 1976, it was readily apparent that Tram was on a fast track to the big leagues. In his only full season of minor-league ball (at Double A Montgomery in 1977), he was named the Southern League's Most Valuable Player.

From the start, though, the Tigers were more than hopeful about Trammell's future. They were genuinely excited about it. But how would he react to being more than gently nudged up the organizational ladder?

Would he be ready for it? The answer was that he would be. Even so, it all happened so fast.

The first Detroit newspaper clipping about Trammell appeared on June 9, 1976, the day after he was drafted in the second round. But he wasn't mentioned in the headline of the story that appeared in the Detroit Free Press.

"Tigers Draft Left-Handed Pitcher" – it read, referring to Pat Underwood, the Tigers' first-round choice.

"He's the type of youngster who won't let you cross the plate," said Bill Lajoie, the Tigers' scouting director. "We think he can reach the majors in two years."

Of Trammell, a scouting report was quoted: "Has good running speed, a good arm, great hands and fine instincts, all the tools to become a major-league regular at shortstop."

But there was no speculation about how long it would take. Therefore, the future was anything but clear. After all, Trammell looked so very young – being just out of high school – not to mention the fact that the Tigers had selected four other shortstops in the draft.

Trammell had a self-confident way about him, though. As he later said, without bragging, "I knew I could play."

Steadily improving at the plate while at Montgomery – and living up to the scouting report defensively – Trammell began looking like a probable call-up at the end of the Southern League's season.

But Montgomery had playoffs to get through first, and a championship to win, before he and his double-play partner Lou Whitaker could be added to the Tigers' roster.

Finally, the day arrived.

The two prospects joined the team in Detroit on a Thursday just minutes before a game against Baltimore. Neither Tram nor Lou got into that game, but when it looked like Tigers' second baseman Tito Fuentes had gotten hurt, Whitaker ran out – almost all the way – to his position before Fuentes signaled that he would remain in the game. Lou returned to the dugout.

Trammell and Whitaker were told they would start the second game of the next night's doubleheader against the Red Sox at Fenway Park. Despite their hope the two of them would do well the

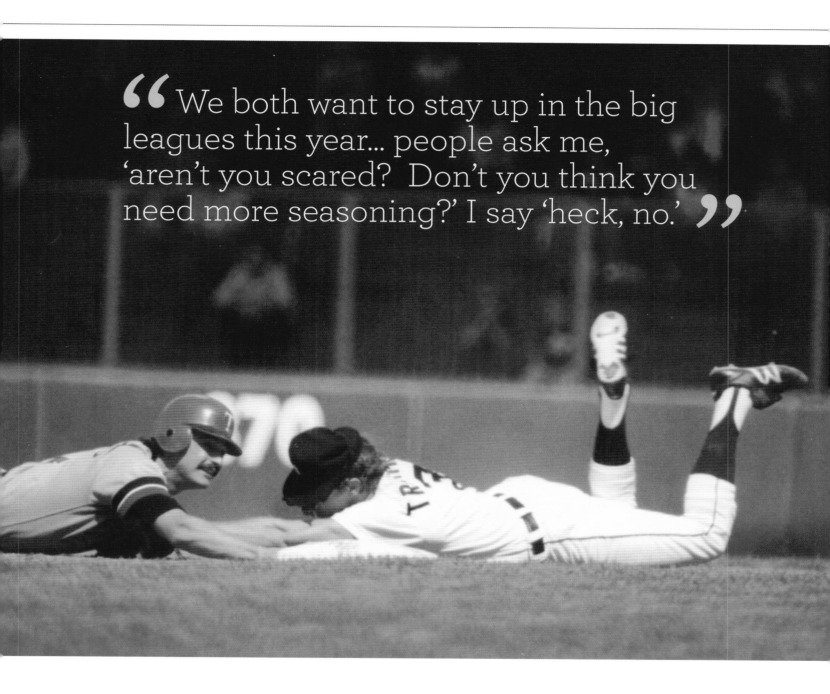

"We both want to stay up in the big leagues this year... people ask me, 'aren't you scared? Don't you think you need more seasoning?' I say 'heck, no.'"

rest of the way, the Tigers couldn't be sure.

"I've seen kids come up at the end of the season and not hit a thing," said Tigers' manager Ralph Houk. "On the other hand, I've seen them come up and hit .450.

"You can't really judge such a short test. All you can do is take the recommendation of those who've seen them over the long haul."

But in an Associated Press report, it was written that "if Trammell and Whitaker aren't outstanding from the beginning, it's bound to be a letdown to the fans who've been led to expect so much."

Even if that meant there would be pressure on him to perform, Trammell immediately embraced the challenge. Of the anticipation the fans were feeling, he said "that makes it better. People know who we are already. I don't think it will hurt us at all."

The next night – making their debut on Sept. 9, 1977 – Trammell singled his first time up against right-hander Reggie Cleveland, as did Whitaker.

It was their way of saying, "hello, Tigers. Hello, big leagues."

The following spring neither player was wide-eyed. Their time with the team in September had helped them over that hurdle.

"We both want to stay up in the big leagues this year," Trammell said. "People ask me, 'aren't you scared? Don't you think you need more seasoning?' I say 'heck, no.'

"I want to play up here right now. We could be a good double-play combination for years to come. But that's just talk; we have to go out and do it."

And so they did. ●

That ball has a chance.

"I've seen kids come up at the end of the season and not hit a thing... On the other hand, I've seen them come up and hit .450."

– TIGERS' MANAGER RALPH HOUK

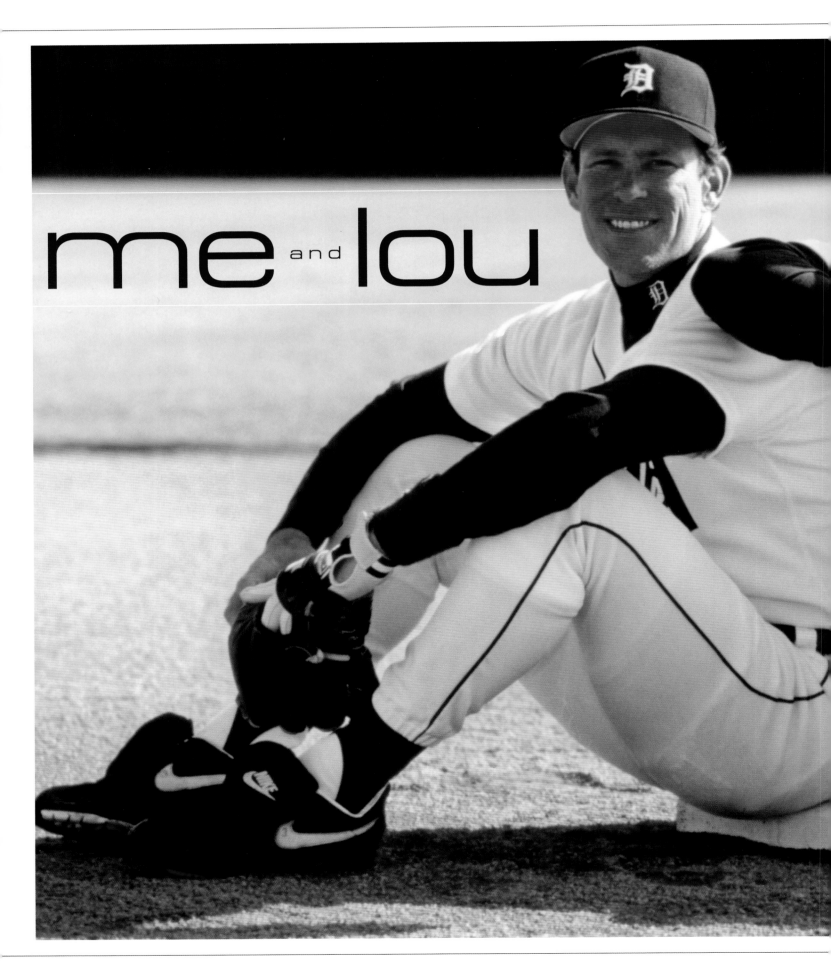

me and lou

chapter five

3
THREE

a salute to
ALAN
TRAMMELL

THEY ENDED UP BEING AS CLOSE AS BROTHERS AND SETTING RECORDS FOR HOW LONG THEY PLAYED TOGETHER.

But, Tram, don't be offended. Lou Whitaker didn't want to be your double-play partner. In the beginning, he didn't want to be anyone's double-play partner.

He wanted to play the position he was happiest at – the position he started at.

Third base.

But the Tigers had other ideas.

When the Tigers drafted Alan Trammell in 1976, soon after which it began to look like he was their shortstop of the future, they were already contemplating a move from third to second base for Whitaker.

But Lou was having such a good season at Lakeland that Jim Leyland, his manager at the time, convinced the Tigers' front office that moving him in 1976 would be too disruptive.

So they waited until the end of the season.

It wasn't a move that Whitaker, who was drafted a year ahead of Trammell, wanted to make.

"I might even have shed a few tears," he said. "My whole life had been at third base, and you're telling me you want to make a second baseman out of me?"

That's exactly what the Tigers were telling him, however. When the 1976 season ended, they sent both Trammell and Whitaker to the Florida Instructional League to work with former Gold Glove shortstop Eddie Brinkman – but

above all, to work together.

They also roomed together and ate together.

"It was like having a shadow," said Whitaker.

"But from the beginning, we clicked," said Trammell.

And that's how the greatest double-play combination in Tigers' history was born.

"One of the reasons it worked so well," said Trammell, "is that there never was any jealousy between us. If anything, it was the opposite. We pulled for each other instead of trying to outshine each other.

"We were always on the same page."

That's because the two of them talked to each other as much on the field as off. Remember how they used to hold their gloves up to their mouths to protect the signals they exchanged?

"It was all about what kind of pitch was going to be thrown and where the ball would likely go if the batter hit it on the ground," said Trammell. "We were also making sure who would cover second on a possible steal.

"I did the talking 90 percent of the time, but I knew Lou well enough that if he disagreed with me, and was adamant about it, I went with it."

Theirs was a relationship based on mutual respect as individuals and professional athletes.

They didn't socialize off the field, as their careers unfolded, but they could not have been closer on it.

Perhaps even more important than their first game together in the majors was the date that they took their positions the following

"One of the reasons it worked so well, is that there never was any jealousy between us. If anything, it was the opposite. We pulled for each other instead of trying to outshine each other."

Whether it was 6-4-3 or 4-6-3, either way worked.

April as starters on Opening Day at Tiger Stadium.

It's one thing to make your debut in an otherwise meaningless September game, knowing that only a few weeks remain to the season. It's entirely different to be out there on the first day of a 162-game schedule.

That's not to say the Tigers just handed them their jobs.

To the extent that the Tigers traded their regular shortstop, Tom Veryzer, and starting second baseman, Tito Fuentes during the off-season, yes, the decks were cleared for the kids, but Trammell was still uncertain how much his closest competitor, Mark Wagner, was going to play in 1978.

Whitaker was in a similar situation at second base with Steve Dillard.

Both of them were confident in their ability to become full-time starters. But they weren't entirely sure how they were going to handle some of the distractions.

What initially fascinated them, for instance, was how much noise an Opening Day crowd of more than 50,000 was going to make at Tiger Stadium.

"I can't imagine what it will be like," said Trammell. "I can't picture it. I bet they'll be noisy as hell."

No wonder he couldn't picture it. The night Trammell reported to Tiger Stadium in 1977 for his first game as a major-leaguer, a crowd of only 1,969 was on hand for the game against Baltimore.

This was going to be different.

"I know those people will all be hollering," said Whitaker. "Maybe I'll have butterflies for a while. But when the game starts, I'll have my stuff together."

With Whitaker and Trammell in the starting lineup, the Tigers beat the Toronto Blue Jays 6-2 behind Mark Fidrych on Opening Day at Tiger Stadium in 1978. They each had a hit; they each scored a run and both of them walked once.

And, oh yes, they turned a 6-4-3 double play.

But even then, there wasn't much difference between them at the plate.

Proving how much they intended to retain their starting jobs, the two enjoyed almost identical Aprils in their first full major-league season. Trammell hit .303; Whitaker hit .306.

By the end of that first month, it wasn't yet guaranteed they'd continue to start, but it looked probable they would.

"Last year (for the final month)," said Trammell, "I felt I was just up here. Now it's like I'm part of the team."

Indeed, he would be part of the team for 20 years – with Lou right beside him.

"Tram and Lou" or "Lou and Tram", no matter how you say it, the two were a tandem. They were a team. ●

Meeting former Tiger shortstop Billy Rogell.

They were magic in the field and dangerous at the plate.

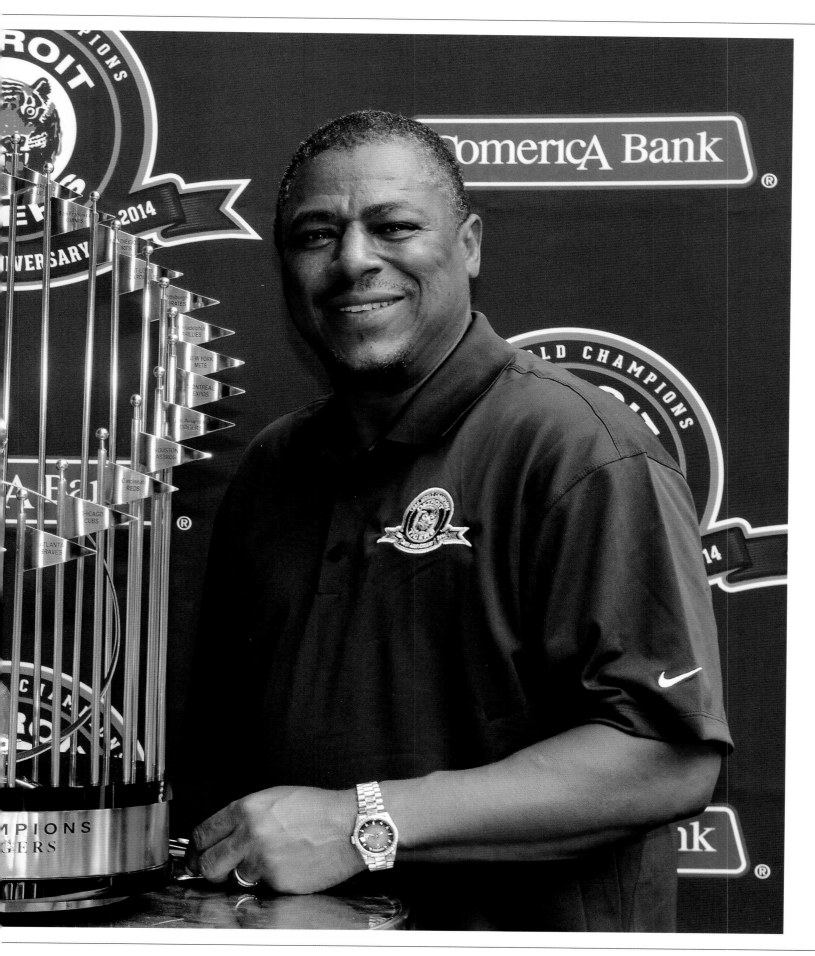

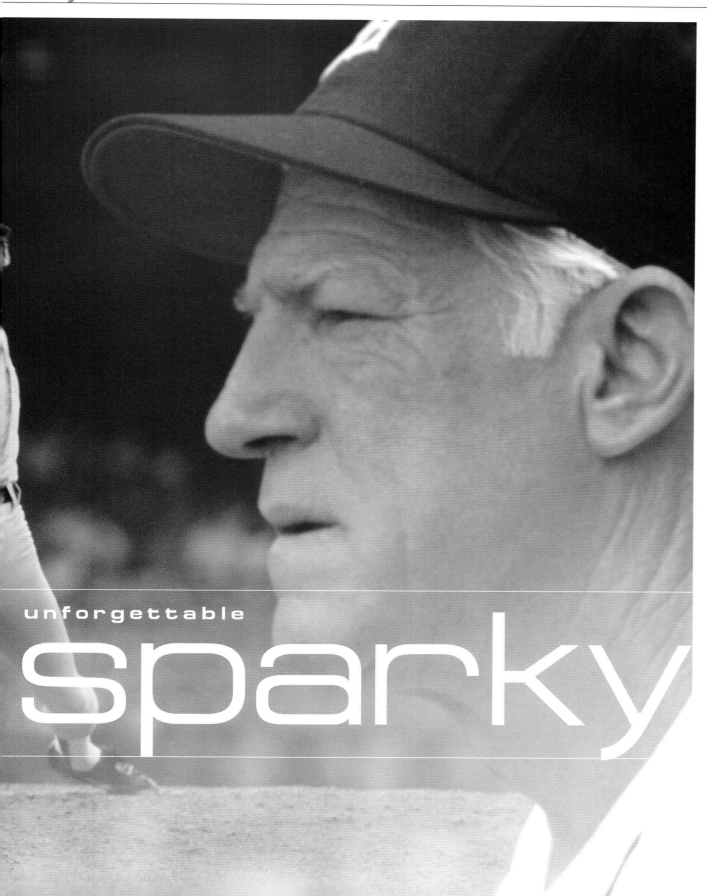

chapter six

3

THREE

a salute to
ALAN
TRAMMELL

unforgettable

sparky

ALAN TRAMMELL WENT THROUGH A WHIRLWIND OF MANAGERS AT THE BEGINNING OF HIS MAJOR-LEAGUE CAREER.

Ralph Houk was his first manager. He's the one who welcomed Tram up from the minors for the last month of the 1977 season – and who made the decision to start him as the Tigers' shortstop in 1978.

"I'd really like to play them as much as I can." Houk said of Trammell and Lou Whitaker upon their promotion from the minors.

Les Moss was his second manager – but lasted only 53 games in 1979. Trammell hadn't yet developed into the player he was to become, but there were already signs he would.

In an analysis that he wrote for the Detroit Free Press in January of that year, Al Kaline said "I do think that if anyone's going to be the team leader, Trammell is going to be the guy.

"A lot of players try to sound confident, but Alan really is."

Never a talkative man, there's no evidence that Moss ever said

"Whatever I do in life, I will use the lessons that Sparky taught us."

"That kid at short is going to be a star".

much about Trammell. He just penciled him in as his starting shortstop. It might have been just a coincidence that Tram hit only .208 in his last 23 games for Moss and .356 in his first 23 for Sparky Anderson.

Then again, it might not have been.

No matter what, Trammell instantly took to Anderson's vibrant approach after initially being stunned by the managerial switch.

"I feel sorry for Les," Alan said. "On this team, we're finding out that anything can happen."

Little did Tram know at the time – "I was intimidated the first time I met him," he said – but Sparky was going to have a profound effect on his life, not just his career. That's because Anderson didn't just take over as his manager; he became his mentor.

Sparky helped build Tram as a player and mold him as a person. Appreciative of both, Trammell's regard and respect for the man steadily climbed.

"Whatever I do in life," Trammell would later say, "I will use the lessons that Sparky taught us."

Those lessons began with not just talking a good game. Anderson didn't like players who "just talk a good game."

But his words about playing baseball "the right way" resonated with the Tigers' 21-year-old short-stop. Anderson said what Tram wanted to hear.

Plus he also liked Anderson's optimism.

"I ain't promising nothin' this year," Sparky said, upon arriving in Detroit. "But we're going to do some winning here. I swear to God we are."

Sparky, a fatherly figure with

Name of the class: Switching Pitchers 101.

Sparky was a live wire - even amoung friends.

"Are you blind? Tram made that tag in time."

> 66 I didn't go to school to pick my nose or eat my lunch. I know what talent is here. I also know what the results can be if they're just willing to work. 99

his silver hair, said that most of the players on his new team looked like "college kids."

Maybe because he was no older than a "college kid" himself, Trammell liked that as well. But mostly, he found Sparky's enthusiasm to be contagious.

Saying that the Tigers had "the finest young talent in the game today", Anderson added, "it will be a tough grind, but if the kids will just believe in me, they can do it.

"I didn't go to school to pick my nose or eat my lunch. I know what talent is here," Anderson said. "I also know what the results can be if they're just willing to work."

No one was more willing to work than Trammell. He believed in Sparky – "we needed him," he said – and the trust was reciprocated. By the time the Tigers won it all

in 1984, Anderson thought that Trammell was the best shortstop in baseball, "but nobody outside Detroit knows it."

"He's the best shortstop I've ever seen."

Trammell knew how to take Anderson's praise in stride, however.

"I know where he's coming from. He talks a lot, most of it from the heart. I appreciate it, but the last thing I think about when I'm taking the field is what Sparky thinks of me."

Make no mistake, the student enjoyed being praised by the teacher, but never lost sight of having to earn it.

For his part, Anderson obviously didn't think Trammell received the praise he deserved. But, surprisingly, he didn't go overboard with shock in 1987 when

Trammell finished second in the MVP voting to Toronto's George Bell.

"Either one could have won it," Sparky said. "It was like flipping a coin and having it come out 50 ½ to 49 ½."

Anderson didn't explain how a coin flip could produce a split point, but sometimes you just smiled and nodded when he made one of his legendary verbal blunders – like when he said that Jose Canseco was "built like a Greek Goddess."

That was Sparky – from his first day in Detroit until his last.

Announcing that "I ain't here no more", Anderson retired from managing after the 1995 season – the same year Whitaker retired. Trammell gave it some thought, but decided to play one more season.

He wanted the record to show that he played 20 years (1977-96) for the same team. But by the end of the '96 season, it was time.

"That's what Sparky said almost a year ago today," Trammell said. "It's time."

They remained in touch – and the manager/player relationship evolved into a deep friendship. When he was a coach for San Diego in 2000, Trammell told the Padres that the only day he wanted off was Sparky's induction day into the Hall of Fame.

As part of a video tribute to his mentor when that day arrived, Trammell said "we needed direction. He was the perfect one to lead us to the Promised Land."

Of the 1984 team, Anderson commented that "they grew up good."

When Sparky died in 2010, Tram sadly said what he still feels.

"I loved the man. I'm not afraid to say it."

He hears you, Tram. Somehow, somewhere, he hears you. ●

One big happy family.

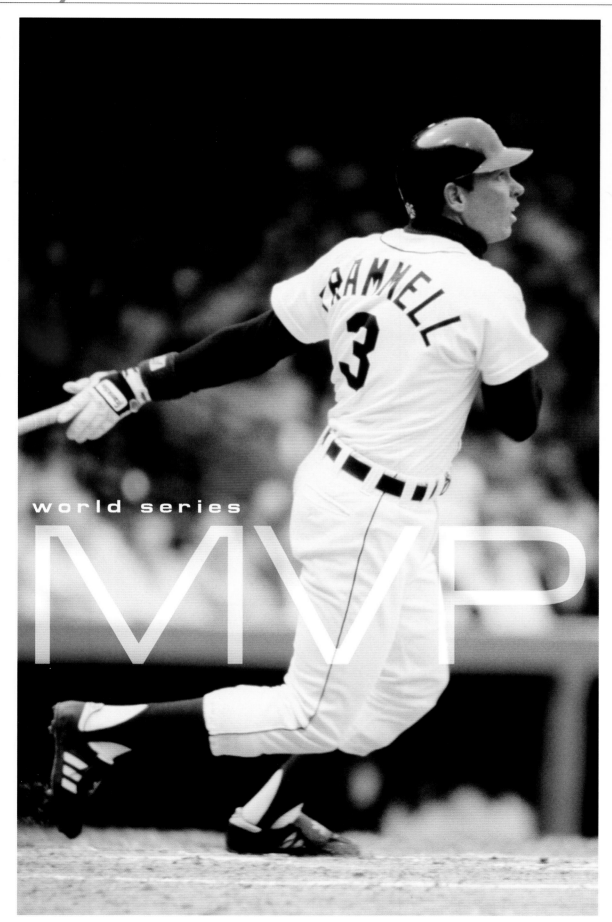

world series

MVP

3
THREE

a salute to
ALAN TRAMMELL

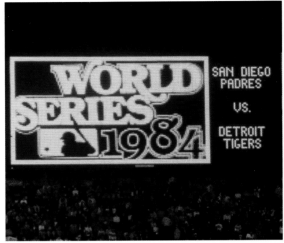

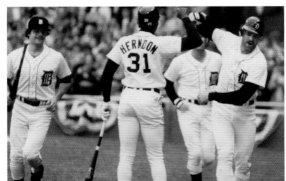

GAME 4 OF THE 1984 WORLD SERIES WAS AS GOOD AS IT GETS FOR ALAN TRAMMELL.

ON SECOND THOUGHT, HE WOULDN'T WANT SUCH INDIVIDUAL CREDIT FOR WHAT WAS A GREAT TEAM ACHIEVEMENT.

As every good Tigers' fan knows or remembers, the Tigers beat the San Diego Padres in five games – thanks to the achievements of many.

Jack Morris' two wins.

Kirk Gibson's memorable home run in Game 5 off Goose Gossage.

Larry Herndon's difference-making home run in Game 1.

Trammell was one of the Tigers' heroes in the World Series of '84. In fact, for his nine hits – among them the two home runs he hit in Game 4 – he was named its Most Valuable Player.

He would require both knee and shoulder surgery within a week of the Series ending, but he starred in it all the same.

Remember Ernie Harwell's classic calls of those home runs, though? Hopefully you do, but keep in mind, they were hit before Ernie punctuated his calls with "long gone!"

"The pitch. . .and here's a drive to left, it's deep. It is waaaaay back and it is gone! A two-run home run by Trammell and a 2-0 lead for the Tigers in the first inning!

"Whitaker scores and here comes Trammell behind him to touch the plate."

Trammell hit that home run on his first at-bat of Game 4. Here's what happened on his second at-bat.

"(Eric) Show ready, kicks and deals. . .here's a swing and there's another drive to left! It's deep and this one is gone, a second home run by Trammell, and the Tigers now lead it 4-1.

"Whitaker scores, here comes Trammell running home, his second consecutive home run. What a series it's been for Alan Trammell!

"They're standing here; they want Trammell to come out and take a curtain call. There he is!"

In his low-key style when it later came to discussing the back-to-back home runs, Tram said "it was a special thrill."

What felt even better, he said, were "all the handshakes from the guys in the dugout."

With a chance to hit yet another home run, Trammell had two more at-bats in Game 4. He singled his next time up, his third hit of the game, and flied out to left in his final at-bat.

Behind Morris, the Tigers won 4-2 to put them in the position of needing only one more victory to

win the series.

"I guess that's the one I'm best remembered for," Trammell said of Game 4. "I can poke the ball once in a while"

But it was not the only game of the five that he should be remembered for.

In Game 1, with his first at-bat in the top of the first inning in San Diego, his hometown, Tram singled in Lou Whitaker from second. He also singled to left in the third and stole second, but was stranded there.

In Game 2, the Tigers took a 3-0 lead in the top of the first with the help of consecutive singles from Whitaker, Trammell and Kirk Gibson.

Trammell scored on Lance Parrish's sacrifice fly in the first, and also singled in the eighth, but their three in the first were the only runs the Tigers scored in a 5-3 loss.

In Game 3, Trammell made it three two-hit games in a row. He doubled in Whitaker for the third run of the Tigers' four-run second and later scored the fourth run of the inning on Herndon's bases-loaded walk.

He also singled in the seventh and walked twice. The Tigers won the game 5-2.

In Game 4, he hit his two home runs, and although he went hitless in Game 5, it was Trammell's sacrifice bunt in the eighth that set up the pivotal showdown between Gibson and Gossage with runners at second and third.

The thought was that Gossage would walk Gibson intentionally with first base open, but the proud Goose didn't want to.

Instead, with the thought he

Sports Illustrated

OCTOBER 22, 1984 $1.95

GRRREAT !

**World Series MVP
Alan Trammell
Of The Tigers**

Singled out by Sports Illustrated for hitting two HR in Game 4 and .450 overall.

A happy handshake from Alex Grammas.

"We didn't want to go back to San Diego" – but we didn't have to.

Going, going... gone!

could strike him out, he pitched to Gibson, who responded by burying the Padres with a three-run home run. It was Gibson's second home run of the game. His first had come in the first inning – with his buddy Trammell on first base after hitting into a fielder's choice.

The outcome served as a textbook example of how to help your team, as Trammell did in the clincher, without getting a hit.

In the five games, Trammell led the Tigers with a .450 batting average (9-for-20), a .500 on-base percentage, an .800 slugging average and a 1.300 OPS.

For being named MVP, he won a Pontiac Trans-Am.

"He was unbelievable," said the Padres' Steve Garvey. "Whitaker and he would get on base, but, of course, sometimes he would decide to just pop one over the fence."

The World Series share that Trammell won didn't mean anything to him. Money wasn't the important prize.

"I won't be able to look at the money 20 years from now," he said. "But I will look at the ring. I'll wear that baby every day for the rest of my life."

That was his intention. It really was. And he wore it a long time before putting it into a safe deposit box for fear of chipping it.

But now that he is in the Hall of Fame, so is his 1984 World Series ring. Look for it in his showcase, if you ever have the opportunity to do so.

"I've donated it," he said. "That's where it will be from now on." ●

“ I won't be able to look at the money
20 years from now, but I will look at the ring.
I'll wear that baby every day for the rest
of my life. ”

Tom Monahan shares World Series trophy with former owner John Fetzer.

chapter eight

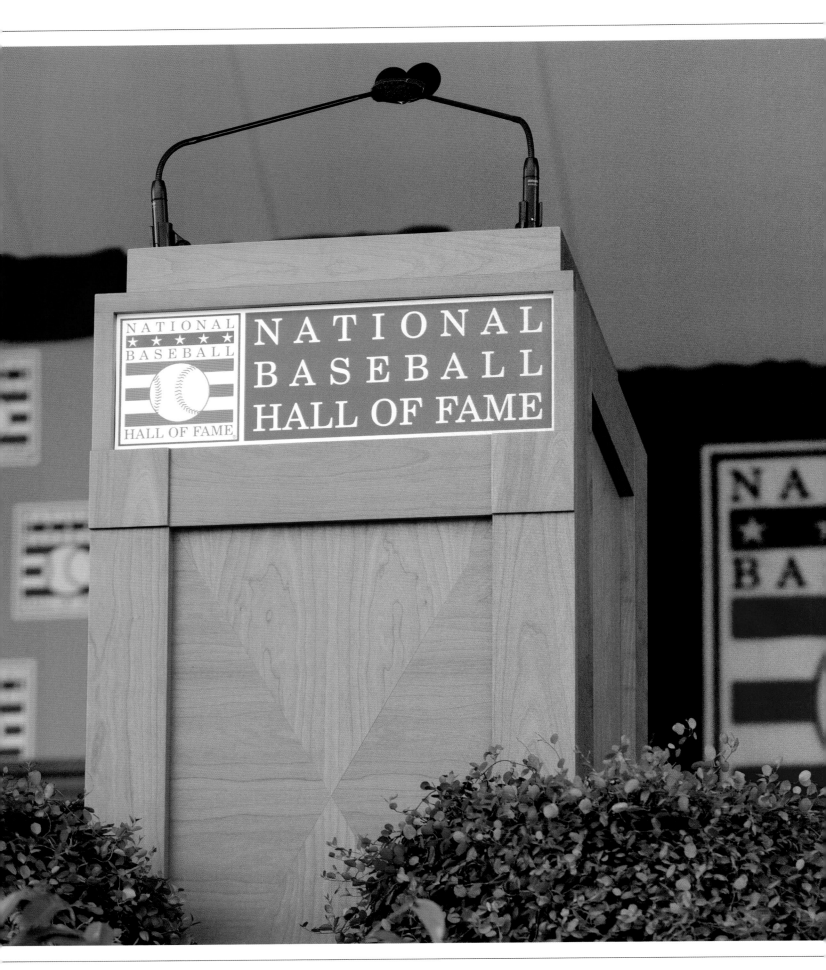

3
THREE

a salute to
ALAN
TRAMMELL

THE ULTIMATE
honor

There they are - the greatest of the greats.

ALAN STUART TRAMMELL
DETROIT, A.L. 1977-96
CATALYST FOR DOMINANT TIGERS TEAMS OF THE 1980S WHO
SHOWCASED ALL-AROUND EXCELLENCE FOR TWO DECADES
AT SHORTSTOP. SIX-TIME ALL-STAR AND WINNER OF FOUR
GOLD GLOVE AWARDS. HIT .300-OR-BETTER IN SEVEN
SEASONS. DEVELOPED POWER LATER IN CAREER TO STEP
INTO CLEAN-UP SLOT, A RARITY FOR MIDDLE INFIELDERS
OF HIS ERA. UPON RETIREMENT, RANKED AMONG TOP 10
SHORTSTOPS ALL-TIME IN HITS, DOUBLES AND HOME RUNS,
AS WELL AS DEFENSIVE GAMES AND FIELDING PERCENTAGE.
NAMED MOST VALUABLE PLAYER OF 1984 WORLD SERIES
AFTER BATTING .450 WITH TWO HOMERS AND SIX RBI IN
DETROIT'S FIVE-GAME VICTORY OVER SAN DIEGO.

AND WHEN THE BIG DAY ARRIVED, HE EMBRACED IT WITH ALL THE STEADINESS THAT HE DEMONSTRATED AS A PLAYER.

Alan Trammell didn't deliver a flashy speech when he was inducted into the National Baseball Hall of Fame.

But you probably didn't expect one.

He didn't reach for laughs by telling a lot of jokes. He didn't wander off in search of extra emotion. There was enough packed into the script as it was.

He didn't even mention by name most of the players who have been his closest friends over the years.

But that's because all his teammates, not just some, have

been important to him. Think about that: Managers have praised Trammell for being the ultimate team player – never putting himself above others, nor favoring a pecking order of importance.

To this day, Trammell is close with many former teammates. But when you have a million friends, how do you thank them all? The answer is you can't.

He was compelled in his speech to talk about Lou Whitaker, of course. The two of them weren't just friends, they were joined at the hip as baseball's longest-existing double play combination.

But Tram didn't overdo his emphasis on Lou. As with most of his throws to first base, he did it just right.

"Lou, it was an honor and a

ALAN STUART TRAMMELL
DETROIT, A.L. 1977-96

CATALYST FOR DOMINANT TIGERS TEAMS OF THE 1980S WHO
SHOWCASED ALL-AROUND EXCELLENCE FOR TWO DECADES
AT SHORTSTOP. SIX-TIME ALL-STAR AND WINNER OF FOUR
GOLD GLOVE AWARDS, HIT .300-OR-BETTER IN SEVEN
SEASONS. DEVELOPED POWER LATER IN CAREER TO STEP
INTO CLEAN-UP SLOT, A RARITY FOR MIDDLE INFIELDERS
OF HIS ERA. UPON RETIREMENT, RANKED AMONG TOP 10
SHORTSTOPS ALL-TIME IN HITS, DOUBLES AND HOME RUNS,
AS WELL AS DEFENSIVE GAMES AND FIELDING PERCENTAGE.
NAMED MOST VALUABLE PLAYER OF 1984 WORLD SERIES
AFTER BATTING .450 WITH TWO HOMERS AND SIX RBI IN
DETROIT'S FIVE-GAME VICTORY OVER SAN DIEGO.

pleasure to have played beside you for all those years," Trammell said.

And it would not have been the speech you'd expect Trammell to make had he not singled out Sparky Anderson, his manager for 17 years - and the person "who had the biggest influence on my career.

"I know he's smiling down on all of us today."

Even while saying that he considered Anderson an "extension of my parents", Tram didn't get maudlin about the man. To over-emote about his mentor would have been out of step with what he wanted to accomplish with the speech.

Tram wanted to be Tram with his speech, nothing more, nothing less. That wasn't his stated intent while he was delivering it, but you could tell. Known as a player you could depend on, he wanted to deliver a speech in the same reliable vein.

But most of all, he wanted to show respect for the moment. While being inducted into the Hall of Fame, you don't suddenly stray from how you've always conducted yourself.

At least not if you're Alan Trammell.

His speech started with an endearing moment, though. As Trammell was reaching for his reading glasses, Tigers' fans in the vast crowd started chanting "let's go, Tigers" – accompanied by rhythmic applause.

"I hear ya," Trammell said with that youthful smile of his. Then he took a deep breath, adjusted the microphones in front of him, and began to deliver the most important speech of his life – one,

however, for which he was consummately prepared.

Just like he'd always been prepared as a ballplayer.

He thanked the hierarchy of the Hall of Fame first – almost as if it were the front office of his newest team. That's because it actually is the front office of his newest team.

That's how Tram set out on his path of respect in his speech. He thanked the Modern Baseball Era committee "for selecting both Jack (Morris) and I. Knowing that the voting committee included many of our peers makes this even sweeter."

As another show of respect, he said he was honored to be entering the Hall of Fame with the five other members of the Class of 2018 – Chipper Jones, Jim Thome, Trevor Hoffman, Vladimir Guerrero and Morris.

He thanked the Ilitch family "not only for what you've done for the Tigers, but what you've brought to the city of Detroit."

Then he turned to "Mr. Tiger" – Al Kaline – and thanked him for "being the role model that you are."

"Tiger fans, I know you're out there," Trammell said next. "Today is as much about you as it is about me. As Ernie Harwell used to say when we turned a double-play, you get two for the price of one with Jack and I going into the Hall of Fame together."

He praised his parents for being "the ones who instilled in me the structure, discipline and preparation that's needed to be successful."

Family introductions were next: His two sisters, Lynne and Nancy, plus his wife Barbara and his children, Lance, Kyle and Jade.

He specifically thanked his wife for being "my biggest supporter, my confidante and the backbone of our family."

And as a nod to how it all began for him with the Tigers in 1976, Trammell credited the late scout Dick Wiencek "for convincing Bill Lajoie, the Tigers' scouting director, to draft a skinny, 165-pound shortstop with no power.

"I remember Dick telling me that if I hit .250 and played good

<blockquote>❝ Tiger fans, I know you're out there, today is as much about you as it is about me. As Ernie Harwell used to say when we turned a double-play, you get two for the price of one with Jack and I going into the Hall of Fame together. ❞</blockquote>

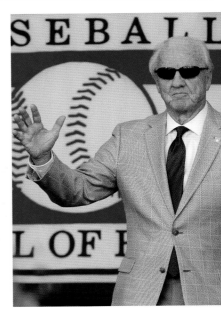

A good time was had by all.

defense, I would play in the big leagues a long time. I doubt that scouts are telling young shortstops that today.

"To all my managers, coaches, trainers, clubhouse personnel and former teammates – many of whom are here today – thank you for being a huge part of this journey. We had so many good times together, and our friendships will be forever."

Tram was humble from start to finish during his speech. You wouldn't have expected anything else.

But it was the way he played and what he accomplished in his career that made this grand occasion happen – and in the end, the achievement itself deserved a nod.

It received the needed credit with a self-acknowledgement of his lofty new status.

"One day, this incredible journey will all sink in." Tram said. "I feel truly honored to now be on baseball's Dream Team."

Gracious all the way through, Trammell thanked "everyone here in Cooperstown and those watching at home for being part of this special day.".

With that, the speech was over. And as if he were backhanding yet another ball in the hole, he'd been flawless. ●

kind words

3
THREE

a salute to
ALAN
TRAMMELL

" Truthfully, I'm as happy as he is... I saw beautiful things, amazing things from Tram. "

F OR A MAN OF SO FEW WORDS, IT'S UNCANNY JUST HOW OFTEN LOU WHITAKER SAYS THE RIGHT ONES.

He has his own way of cutting to the chase – his own history of being perfectly succinct. And once again he has been exactly that.

When Lou appeared on the National Baseball Hall of Fame's video introduction to Alan Trammell's induction speech, it was not the first time he has said about the honor "truthfully, I'm as happy as he is."

But there couldn't have been a better time for him to say it – because in front of a crowd of more 50,000 in Cooperstown, N.Y., Lou merely stated what so many others were thinking.

Everyone who's ever known Tram had to be as happy as he was that day. But mostly they were happy for him.

And when Lou added that "I saw beautiful things, amazing things from Tram", he poignantly summarized the way No. 3 played his position during their 19 years together.

To be inducted into the Hall of Fame and to have your Tigers' uniform number retired within a month of each other are indeed great honors for Trammell.

Maybe someday it will happen for Whitaker as well, now that there have been ceremonies for No. 3 and Jack Morris' No. 47.

Meanwhile, here are more kind words, Tram, from those who admired you as a player – and still admire you as a person.

JOHN SMOLTZ

> "Remember, I grew up a huge Tigers' fan. I wore Alan Trammell's No. 3 in high school. I just loved watching him."

LANCE PARRISH

> " But he's been such a great friend. That's never wavered. As a testament to our friendship, he named one of his sons Lance. I appreciated it then. I appreciate it still. "

Tram has become a lifelong friend.

Our journey together began in 1976 when he came up to Double A Montgomery because we needed a shortstop. He was skinny, but we were all skinny back then. I was being recruited to play both baseball and football, and he was being recruited for baseball, but I didn't find out until later that we both signed letters of intent to play at UCLA.

We would have been teammates at UCLA if we hadn't both signed with the Tigers.

I give Tram a lot of credit, because he does a heck of a job keeping in contact with everybody. Like he never forgets my birthday and I know he stays in touch with a lot of other guys from 1984. I don't know how long the list is, but he's very good at that. He's kind of the camp coordinator.

Tram was all baseball, though. His life revolved around it. Always talking about it, always reading about it. I think he's read everything that's ever been written about baseball. You could throw almost any question at him, and he would know the answer. It was amazing.

He'd sit on the plane reading baseball publications from cover to cover – and I don't think he's ever watched a TV show other than Sports Center. He's a sport junkie. That's just Tram.

But he's been such a great friend. That's never wavered. As a testament to our friendship, he named one of his sons Lance. I appreciated it then. I appreciate it still.

He's just a great person to be around – and a great human being. But if I could add one thing, just from a baseball perspective, I watched Tram evolve from someone who was a decent hitter and a pretty good shortstop into a player who almost was a Most Valuable Player with clean-up like numbers in 1987.

Not too bad for a skinny little shortstop.

Come to think of it, even when I try to remember him screwing up a play, I can't.

JACK MORRIS

I REMEMBER MY FIRST IMPRESSION OF TRAM PROMPTED ME TO ASK HIM "WHERE ARE YOU FROM? CALIFORNIA?"

He had longer hair, not super-long, but long. So I asked him "Are you a surfer? And he started laughing.

"No, I just play baseball," he replied.

I had no clue then that we would ever win a World Series, let alone everything else we've gone on to – such as the Hall of Fame. Back then, we were just trying to stay at Double A.

But it didn't take me long to realize that Tram was a talented defensive player. He could pick it, he could throw and he was accurate. He didn't have the strongest arm, but the runner never won.

And I knew that because of his work ethic, his hitting would come around – which it did.

He's been like a brother to me. Always will be.

> " He's been like a brother to me. Always will be. "

TREVOR HOFFMAN

"He's just a great example of what it means to have class – to be a true professional."

I COULDN'T GET OVER HIS ENERGY AS A COACH FOR THE SAN DIEGO PADRES, HIS TENACITY TO WIN, HIS COMPETITIVE SPIRIT. TRAM HAS BEEN A GREAT SOURCE OF ENTHUSIASM TO ME. IT'S SOMETHING THAT RUBBED OFF ON ME AND I TOOK TO HEART.

He never doubted the player that he was. He never held a grudge about the Hall of Fame process. He's just a great example of what it means to have class – to be a true professional.

I think Detroit was lucky to have him for 20 years.

DAN DICKERSON

What comes to mind isn't just his day-to-day reliability, but his overall excellence.

As a young fan I don't think I truly appreciated how good he was, but I sure loved watching him. Maybe he didn't make spectacular diving stops, but, man, did he make plays.

I'm still mad he didn't win the MVP award in 1987. For one of the greatest seasons ever by a shortstop, it's just a shame Tram didn't get rewarded for it by being named MVP.

I remember going to the last game that he and Lou played together at Tiger Stadium in 1995. I took a little camera with me. It didn't have much of a lens, so the two of them were just two little dots on the photos I took.

But, by golly, I wanted to record the moment because I knew we'd probably never again see two guys playing together for that long.

I admired him as a manager, too. He approached everything the same way he always did as a player - with endless enthusiasm. Even now, in his front office role, he wants to be on the field.

Here is this Hall of Famer wanting to sit with young players in the minors and offer whatever that youngster needs to realize his full potential. It's just so much fun to see.

I'm so impressed with the career Tram had, but also with the person that he is. He loves what he does – spreading his love of the game to the next generation of ballplayers.

> " By golly, I knew we'd probably never again see two guys playing together for that long. "

> " I'm so impressed with the career Tram had, but also with the person that he is. He loves what he does – spreading his love of the game to the next generation of ballplayers. "

TOM BROOKENS

YOU'RE GOING TO HEAR THIS FROM MORE GUYS THAN JUST ME, BUT TRAM IS A SPORTS NUT.

He's been as good a friend as I have ever had in baseball, but when we were teammates, we'd go out for breakfast, and he'd never say a word.

He'd be holding the newspaper in front of his face the whole time. Yeah, we'd go out to eat, but it was like eating alone.

Next on my list to tell you is that despite that innocent smile, Tram was an instigator when it came to the clubhouse. In a good-natured way, he'd be at the bottom of a lot of mischief that went on. Something would happen, and because of that laugh of his, you just knew you'd eventually be thinking, "Tram, you're at the bottom of this."

It wasn't ever anything serious. He just knew how to keep a team loose. Like all the trivia questions he used to ask us. Man, he loved trivia.

Those were great days to be a Tiger. He and Lou would get on base and bing-bang-boom, someone would drive them in At that point, it would be 'game on', we're ahead."

As I said, those were great days.

> " He and Lou would get on base and bing-bang-boom, someone would drive them in. At that point, it would be 'game on', we're ahead... those were great days. "

TONY LARUSSA

❝ I've made no secret of how much I have admired him. He was as good as anyone who played in our generation. He was the perfect player. ❞

They drilled him.

I got really pissed off. I picked Trammell to retaliate against. LaMarr Hoyt brushed him back a couple of times. Well, that led to a lot of comments. Someone called me a minor-league punk.

When we next went to Detroit, there was a lot of talk in the papers about bad blood and predictions about trouble. I was worried about what might happen.

But nothing did because Sparky and I had a good relationship - and because Tram didn't make a big deal about it.

He reacted with class to everything. As I said, he ranks as my favorite opposing player.

YOU CAN ASK AROUND – OVER THE LAST 30-SOME YEARS, I'VE TOLD EVERYBODY FOREVER THAT MY FAVORITE OPPOSING PLAYER WAS ALAN TRAMMELL.

I was a lousy infielder with a sore arm, so I enjoyed going out to the dugout early just to watch him take groundballs. He was just so sure, so smooth – and his arm was true.

Plus you could put him anywhere in the lineup – leadoff, second, third or fourth – and he would deliver. His ego was always in check; he didn't draw attention to himself; he was a total team man.

I've made no secret of how much I have admired him. He was as good as anyone who played in our generation. He was the perfect player.

A lot of people reacted like I did when he was elected to the Hall of Fame. We celebrated.

Yes, there was an incident once when I managed the White Sox and I remember it like it was yesterday. Steve Kemp was having a big weekend at home for us against his former team, the big, bad Tigers, so in one of his at-bats they knocked him on his ass.

DAVE DOMBROWSKI

Tram's ability on the field always spoke for itself. No matter who you were rooting for, or working for, you had to love his every-day energy for the game.

Not to mention that he's one of the nicest people I've ever met in my life.

He's liked and respected by everyone everywhere in the game of baseball.

" **He's one of the nicest people I've ever met in my life.** "

DARRELL EVANS

We kidded each other so much. I used to tell him I could catch his throws to first base without a glove. He'd laugh. But he always took it the right away because he was so darn accurate.

From the moment I joined the Tigers, the two of us were close – having done some similar things as kids. I was glad to find someone other than me who used to sneak into the nearest ballpark to watch baseball.

Tram snuck into Padres' games as a kid, I snuck into ballparks in Los Angeles.

We were 11 years apart in age, but Tram was just like me. I don't know if he studied the Baseball Encyclopedia like I did, but I wouldn't be surprised if he did.

" **I was glad to find someone other than me who used to sneak into the nearest ballpark to watch baseball.** "

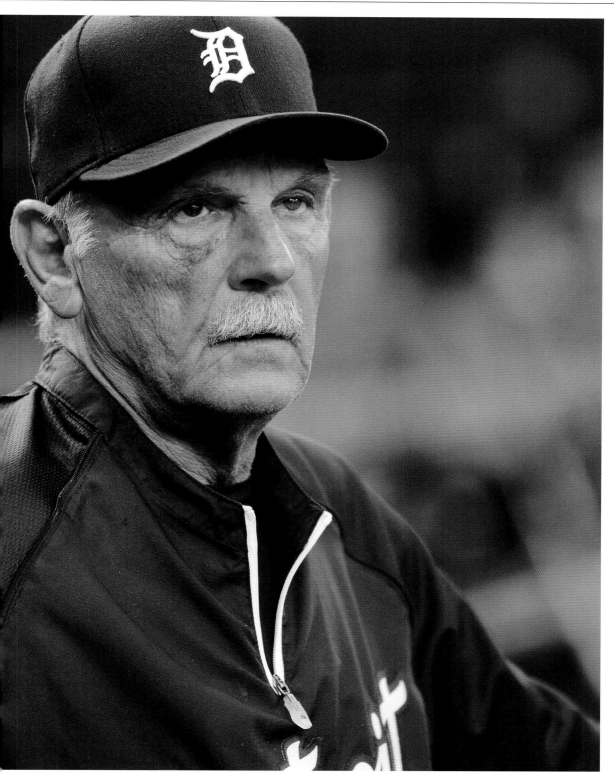

JIM LEYLAND

He never big-leagued anybody although you could tell he was going to be a star. He treated everyone with the utmost respect – like gold, really – me included.

He made you feel important. And he doesn't just work with guys who are supposed to be prospects. He works with everyone he can.

I mean if you look up the definition of a ball player in the dictionary, you should see a photo of Alan Trammell. He's a Hall of Famer who is still giving back to the game and to the Tigers' organization.

It wasn't easy for me to replace him as manager of the Tigers. He was a huge figure in Detroit. But he treated it with total dignity, never any animosity. I can't tell you just how highly I think of him.

People say he had a natural instinct for the game. I call it having a smell for the game. He had a smell for the game – knowing he could happen, what should happen, and how to be in the right place at the right time.

When you are a talented player and have an extra ingredient like that, it makes you a star player.

But he's more than that now because he's a Hall of Famer- where he belongs. It's an honor to know him. He's a Tiger through and through.

> " People say he had a natural instinct for the game. I call it having a smell for the game. "

JIM PRICE

I ONCE INTRODUCED HIM TO A GROUP OF PEOPLE BY SAYING "THIS IS ALAN TRAMMELL. HE'S A BASEBALL PLAYER" AND HE SAID "THANK YOU, THAT'S THE BEST COMPLIMENT I'VE EVER HAD."

There are a lot of guys who play baseball, but Tram is a pure baseball player. He was so fundamentally strong. Never came close to being a hot dog.

I'm telling you, there was no mustard on him at all. He played the game the way it should be played.

All the little things that they have big meetings about now came naturally to him. And at the bat, I'm telling you, he could hurt you. You saw greatness every day when he played.

Both he and Lou came a long way – because when they first came up, they looked like they needed to be fed. But the natural ability in them really showed up.

> " He was so fundamentally strong. Never came close to being a hot dog. I'm telling you, there was no mustard on him at all. He played the game the way it should be played. "

KIRK GIBSON

I'VE SPENT MORE TIME IN
MY LIFE TALKING BASEBALL
WITH TRAM THAN WITH
ANYBODY ELSE I KNOW. WE
REALLY ABSORBED A LOT OF
THE SAME TRAITS FROM OUR
MENTORS. OUR TRUST IN
EACH OTHER IS UNMATCHED.

We spent so much time together,
going to the park, being at the
park, then wrapping up before
leaving the park. I think you can
say we kind of know each other.

My wife used to call Tram my
"road wife" because of how much
time we spent together – and he is,
to this day.

He's a man of such great
integrity that no one can argue,
based on any criteria, against him
being in the Hall of Fame. It's
where he belongs.

He's always been truthful with
me even if it meant telling me I
was wrong. That's still the case.

This will tell you what I think
of him: How many people do you
know that you 100 percent trust?
Not too many, I imagine.

I would trust Alan Trammell
with everything that I have.

> " My wife used to call Tram my
> "road wife" because of how much time
> we spent together – and he is, to this
> day. "

DAN PETRY

I F YOU RECALL, 1981 WAS A STRIKE YEAR FOR BASEBALL – THE SEASON WAS KIND OF PATCHED TOGETHER BEFORE AND AFTER A WORK STOPPAGE.

I was doing O.K., but late in the season, after a tough loss, Tram asked out loud in the clubhouse, "hey, who's pitching for us tomorrow?' When he heard that I was, he replied by saying, "good!"

I overheard him and it gave me a huge boost. I thought to myself, "wow, Alan Trammell says he likes the team's chances when I'm out there."

Well, that just put me over the top confidence-wise. I never forgot it – and I went out there and pitched a whale of a game the next day.

He's meant so much to me. I don't think he ever really knew how much. I remember telling my wife "nobody better ever mess with Tram because they'll have to go through me first."

I guarantee you, I wasn't the only one who felt like that. I remember when we got into an altercation with the White Sox (in 1982) and LaMarr Hoyt came close to hitting Tram three times in the same game, there were guys ready to go after both Hoyt and manager Tony LaRussa.

Indeed, Lance Parrish said that day of LaRussa "he'll be the first to go down. He better run out there with the big guys.

"Cooler heads prevailed, but that's how angry we were with the Sox just for messing with Tram. That's what I mean about how much he meant to us.

"Plus you don't get any better as a person than Tram. You just don't."

> " He's meant so much to me. I don't think he ever really knew how much. I remember telling my wife "nobody better ever mess with Tram because they'll have to go through me first. "

MARIO IMPEMBA

I SKIPPED CLASS AT MICHIGAN STATE TO GO TO GAME 4 OF THE 1984 WORLD SERIES AT TIGER STADIUM. MY BROTHER AND I WERE SITTING IN THE BLEACHERS IN LEFT-CENTER FIELD.

There had been a lottery for the right to buy tickets. I remember getting a letter that said "congratulations, you can purchase two tickets."

It was a cold day, but we were thrilled to be there. I was a big Trammell fan because he was such a fundamentally strong shortstop.

Sometimes you have to be careful what you wish for, though, because your heroes could turn out to be jerks. It's been known to happen. But that's never been the case with Tram, not even close.

He's lived up to everything I ever envisioned he was as a person. What a great guy.

So the World Series game I went to was the one in which he hit two home runs. It doesn't get better than that, does it? I flunked the class I skipped, but oh well.

CRAIG MONROE

HE'S ONE OF THE MOST HUMBLE SUPERSTARS I'VE EVER BEEN AROUND.

He cares about you not only as a baseball player, but as a person – a guy you'd want to run through a wall for.

And I almost did.

RON GARDENHIRE

THE FIRST TIME I EVER GOT TO SEE THE TWO OF THEM, TRAM AND LOU, PLAY ON THE FIELD WAS WHEN I WAS THE THIRD-BASE COACH FOR THE MINNESOTA TWINS.

Being a middle infielder myself when I played, I can honestly say they were amazing to watch – because the two of them always knew each step the other one was going to take.

All it took was for them to glance at each and they knew. I know that's all it took because, as a third base coach, I had to watch them.

But that's really something special when you see two guys who know each other that well.

> " I can honestly say they were amazing to watch – because the two of them always knew each step the other one was going to take. "

BRAD AUSMUS

I'VE BEEN FORTUNATE ENOUGH TO COME FULL CIRCLE WITH TRAM – FROM LISTENING TO HIS FIRST GAME ON THE RADIO WHEN HE GOT CALLED UP, TO BEING HIS TEAMMATE IN 1996 WHEN HE GOT HIS LAST HIT.

I grew up a Red Sox fan in Connecticut. I was seven years old at the time and I remember the radio announcer saying that Tram and Lou were going to be the Tigers' middle-infield combo of the future for Detroit. It was quite prophetic.

Nineteen years later, there he was at first base after the last hit of his career and I'm his teammate watching it all take place.

I remember what an emotional moment it was for everyone when he spoke to the crowd after that game. We respected him so much. That 1996 Tigers' team was pretty young and he was clearly the elder statesman.

But most of us were in awe of his humility – and how great of a career he'd had. Not to mention how long it had lasted.

Fans and colleagues alike respect how he played, and they like him as a human being. He's just a genuine good guy.

One other memory I can share. We lived close to each other in San Diego. He and his wife Barb would come over to our house for Christmas parties. We'd often stop by his house.

I never got him to surf, however. I don't think it was in his blood.

But I vividly remember stopping by Tram's house with another friend and Barb saying he was "out back." We cut through the house, and there he was

> **" I remember what an emotional moment it was for everyone when he spoke to the crowd after that game. We respected him so much. That 1996 Tigers' team was pretty young and he was clearly the elder statesman. "**

studying the Tigers' roster because it was the day before he was flying out to interview for the Tigers managerial job.

Tram is one of the best people I've ever been around in the game.

And to top it off, speaking of coming full circle, I was on the flight with him from San Diego to Orlando for the winter meetings when he got the call from the Hall of Fame.

We were waiting for him by the luggage carrousel when he showed up to get his bag. In fact, we were the first group that he told he'd gotten in.

I really enjoyed being there for that. You could tell from the moment we saw him that he'd gotten good news. His smile said it all.

Tram and friends after he received the call from the HOF and deplaned to the 2017 Baseball Winter Meetings.
Back Row: Steve Boggs, Bud Black, John Boggs, Alan Trammell Trevor Hoffman, Bruce Bochy, Front Row: Brad Ausmus

TERRY FRANCONA

MY FIRST YEAR AS A MAJOR LEAGUE COACH WITH DETROIT WAS TRAM'S LAST YEAR AS A PLAYER.

I remember how he treated me. He probably had forgotten more baseball than I knew, but he always gave you respect.

He endeared himself to everybody, just like he endeared himself to Detroit fans for all those years.

> " He endeared himself to everybody, just like he endeared himself to Detroit fans for all those years. "

who's number  ?

3

THREE

a salute to
ALAN
TRAMMELL

Charlie Gehringer wore No. 3 for only one year, then changed to No. 2.

Mickey Cochrane

Dick McAuliffe

Gary Sutherland

THERE HAVE BEEN MANY PLAYERS WHO HAVE WORN NO. 3 ON THE TIGERS, OF COURSE – BUT ONLY ONE WHO WILL FOREVER BE REMEMBERED AS "NO. 3." ALAN TRAMMELL.

There have also been many fine players who've worn No. 3 in the majors, but only one of them– indeed, only one who's now a Hall of Famer – wore it for 19 of his 20 years on the same team.

Alan Trammell.

Make no mistake, some good players have worn No. 3 through the years for the Tigers, even a couple of great players – including Trammell, whose career has now been celebrated by having the Tigers retire his number.

But did you know that another Hall of Famer, Charlie Gehringer, wore No. 3 for a season before switching to his famous No. 2 that was retired in 1983.

Charlie Gehringer (left) and Mickey Cochrane (right) in the dugout.

In fact, Gehringer was the team's first No 3.

In all, 20 Tigers have worn No. 3. Trammell was the 18th, but he became so well known for wearing it that his number went unused for 11 years while the Tigers waited to see if he would be elected to the Hall of Fame.

Gary Sheffield became the first Tiger following Trammell's retirement in 1996 to wear it. He did so in 2007-2008 – followed by Ian Kinsler, who wore No. 3 for four years.

Kinsler, to his credit, asked Trammell if he could wear it after learning that the number 5 he'd had for eight years with Texas was retired by the Tigers because Hank Greenberg had worn it.

Tito Fuentes

Ferris Fain   Pedro Garcia

Gary Sheffield

Alan Kinsler

"I have no problem with it at all," Trammell replied. "I hope he gets plenty of hits in it."

Elsewhere, Harold Baines wore No. 3 for 22 years, most of them (but not 19 like Trammell) for the Chicago White Sox. Hall-of-Famer Harmon Killebrew wore No. 3 for 19 years, but spent some of those seasons playing for the Washington Senators before they moved to Minnesota.

Dale Murphy wore No. 3 for 18 years, most of them, but not all, for the Atlanta Braves – and before Trammell, Dick McAuliffe wore it for 16 years, all but the last two for the Tigers.

The scrappy McAuliffe finished out his career as No. 3 for the Boston Red Sox.

Other notable No. 3's included former Tigers' manager Phil Garner (14 years), Hall of Famer Jimmie Foxx (12 years) and Alex Rodriguez, 10 years for Seattle and Texas before he switched to No. 13 with the New York Yankees because No. 3 (Babe Ruth's number) was retired.

Ruth, truth be told, only wore it as a Yankee for six years (1929-34) because uniforms were number-less before that.

But whenever it'll be asked by future generations of Tigers' fans, "who was No. 3?" it will be answered in unison:

"Alan Trammell". ●

Eddie Mayo (above), Chick King (below)

Who's worn No. 3 for the Tigers?

1931 CHARLIE GEHRINGER
1932-33 JOHN STONE
1934-37 MICKEY COCHRANE

1938 CHET LAABS
1939-41 FRANK CROUCHER
1942-43 JIMMY BLOODWORTH
1944-48 EDDIE MAYO

1949-52 JOHNNY GROTH

1953-54 WALT DROPO
1955 FERRIS FAIN
1956 CHICK KING
1957-60 JOHNNY GROTH
1960-73 DICK McAULIFFE
1961 CHUCK COTTIER

1974-76 GARY SUTHERLAND
1976 PEDRO GARCIA
1977 TITO FUENTES
1978-96 ALAN TRAMMELL

2007-08 GARY SHEFFIELD

2014-17 IAN KINSLER

1920
1930
1940
1950
1960
1970
1980
1990
2000
2010
2020

WORTH

Alan Trammell
MODEL

During his last professional game, September 29, 1996, Alan Trammell went 2-for-4 at the plate and, flawless in four chances on the field, wore this cap while turning the final double play of his stellar career.
Loaned by Alan Trammell

For winning the 1984 World Series MVP Award, Alan Trammell also earned a maroon Pontiac Trans Am from *Sport* magazine. Trammell kept this personalized license plate after he sold the car.
Loaned by Alan Trammell

MICHIGAN
WS MVP
GREAT LAKES

Alan Trammell swung this bat to hit a two-run homer in Game Four of the 1984 World Series. In that game, he smacked a pair of two-run round-trippers (driving in longtime teammate Lou Whitaker both times), accounted for all four of Detroit's runs in the 4-2 victory over the Padres, and lifted the Tigers to a 3-1 Series lead.
Donated by Alan Trammell and the Detroit Tigers

Alan Trammell donned this jersey in 1987, when he was the AL Most Valuable Player runner-up and posted a personal-best 205 hits, 28 home runs, 105 RBI, .343 batting average, and 329 total bases. Trammell led the Tigers to 98 wins, an AL East Division title, and their last postseason appearance for nearly 20 years.
Loaned by Alan Trammell

TRAMMELL
3

For his 1984 World Series performance leading to the Tigers' victory, Alan Trammell earned this MVP trophy and World Series ring. On baseball's biggest stage, he hit .450 with two homers, drove in six, scored five runs, and stole a base in Detroit's five-game triumph over San Diego.
Loaned by Alan Trammell

Alan Trammell received this glove in 1967 for his 10th birthday, then put it to use in San Diego's Cabrillo Little League. "I played shortstop and pitcher during my Little League days, and shortstop was always my favorite," he recalled.
Loaned by Alan Trammell

This ball was used in the game of September 13, 1995, when shortstop Alan Trammell and his second base partner Lou Whitaker set a new AL mark for most games played together (1,915). They both debuted September 9, 1977, and for most games together in the majors.

After his playing career ended, Alan Trammell has continued giving back to baseball. In 2017 he was tapped as a coach for Team USA in the World Baseball Classic, where he earned this gold medal for helping the club win its first WBC championship.

chapter eleven

^{IN} good company

3
THREE

a salute to
ALAN
TRAMMELL

JOHN SCOTT MORRIS
"JACK"
DETROIT, A.L. 1977-90; MINNESOTA, A.L. 1991;
TORONTO, A.L. 1992-93; CLEVELAND, A.L. 1994

INTENSE COMPETITOR WITH A SPIRITED DRIVE AND DETERMINATION WHO
PROPELLED HIS TEAMS AS STAFF ACE. THREE-TIME 20-GAME WINNER AND
FIVE-TIME ALL-STAR HARNESSED SPLIT-FINGERED FASTBALL TO BECOME
WINNINGEST PITCHER OF THE 1980S. WON 19 REGULAR SEASON GAMES –
ND EACH OF HIS THREE POSTSEASON APPEARANCES – FOR DETROIT'S
984 JUGGERNAUT. DURABLE WORKHORSE TOTALED 175 COMPLETE GAMES,
OST OF ANY PITCHER SINCE 1975, AND MADE RECORD 14 STRAIGHT
ENING DAY STARTS. WINNER OF FOUR WORLD CHAMPIONSHIP RINGS
THREE CLUBS. EARNED 1991 WORLD SERIES M.V.P. HONORS,
VING MINNESOTA TO TITLE WITH 10-INNING SHUTOUT IN GAME 7.

ALAN STUART TRAMMELL
DETROIT, A.L. 1977-96

CATALYST FOR DOMINANT TIGERS TEAMS OF THE 1980S WHO
SHOWCASED ALL-AROUND EXCELLENCE FOR TWO DECADES
AT SHORTSTOP. SIX-TIME ALL-STAR AND WINNER OF FOUR
GOLD GLOVE AWARDS. HIT .300-OR-BETTER IN SEVEN
SEASONS. DEVELOPED POWER LATER IN CAREER TO STEP
INTO CLEAN-UP SLOT, A RARITY FOR MIDDLE INFIELDERS
OF HIS ERA. UPON RETIREMENT, RANKED AMONG TOP 10
SHORTSTOPS ALL-TIME IN HITS, DOUBLES AND HOME RUNS,
AS WELL AS DEFENSIVE GAMES AND FIELDING PERCENTAGE.
NAMED MOST VALUABLE PLAYER OF 1984 WORLD SERIES
AFTER BATTING .450 WITH TWO HOMERS AND SIX RBI IN
DETROIT'S FIVE-GAME VICTORY OVER SAN DIEGO.

You don't need all of your hands and feet – like you do with the New York Yankees - to count the uniform numbers that have been retired by the Tigers.

But now you need eight fingers – or toes.

That's because the numbers of Alan Trammell and Jack Morris have been added to the six that previously were retired.

What Tigers were already in the exclusive club?

HERE'S THE LIST.
AL KALINE – NO. 6
CHARLIE GEHRINGER – NO. 2
HANK GREENBERG – NO 5
HAL NEWHOUSER – NO. 16
WILLIE HORTON – NO. 23
SPARKY ANDERSON – NO. 11

Kaline's ceremony in 1980 was the first. But if you are wondering why there wasn't one for Ty Cobb's number, it's because Cobb never wore a number for the Tigers. So,

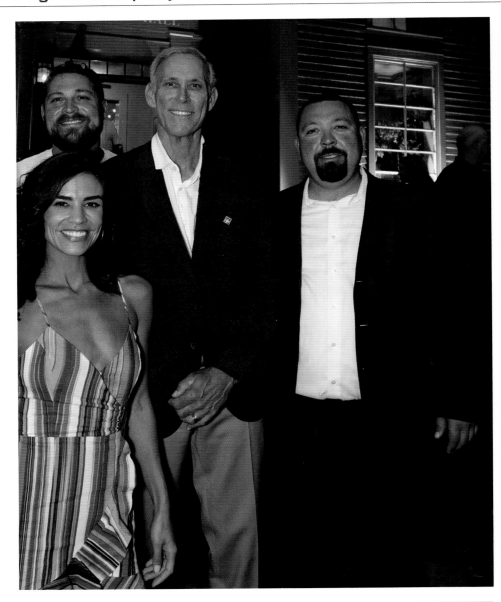

Tram with family and former teammates.

only his name is on the wall.

Neither did Harry Heilmann – nor Sam Crawford.

In fact, there's no record of the Tigers using numbered uniforms until 1931. It just wasn't mandatory yet. Some clubs wore them, some clubs did not.

But congratulations Jack and Tram. You're in good company. Here's how the Tigers' first six number-retirement ceremonies went.

Aug. 17, 1980

Just a few weeks after delivering his Hall-of-Fame induction speech, Kaline stood near home plate at Tiger Stadium, saying what it had meant to him to have worn No. 6.

"Many players take their uniforms for granted. I never did. Every time I put on the Tigers' uniform, I did it with pride."

And for being a Tiger his entire career, Kaline said, "it made it more enjoyable than any player has a right to expect."

Few people remember that when Kaline first became a Tiger in 1953, he wore No. 25, but he was No. 6 by the next season.

And ever since, he's been known as "6".

The day that "6" was retired.

> " Many players take their uniforms for granted. I never did. Every time I put on the Tigers' uniform, I did it with pride. "

June 12, 1983

The two of them had retired decades before, but finally it was happening: Charlie Gehringer and Hank Greenberg were having their numbers retired – No. 2 for Gehringer, No. 5 for Greenberg – on the same day.

"I was surprised they ever did it at all because the Tigers had some great players who never wore numbers," said Gehringer, a man of few words – but always well-chosen words.

In this case, he was referring to Hall-of-Famers Cobb, Heilmann and Crawford, among others.

"I'm sure that's why they hesitated so long," said Gehringer, whom Ernie Harwell called "the epitome of grace and consistency."

Not everything always went right for "The Mechanical Man", however. "I'd go home after a bad day and find my mother on the back porch," he said.

"What's the matter?" she'd say. "Aren't you trying anymore?"

Gehringer and Greenberg were honored on the same day.

June 12, 1983

Greenberg was genuinely moved by having his number retired. After all, he owed his career to the Tigers, after his hometown New York Giants had turned him down.

"I grew up a Giants' fan as most of the kids in New York were, because they had the best team in those days," he reminisced. "I tried to get a tryout with them, but they sent back word that they'd seen me play and I didn't have a chance to make it.

"They wouldn't even let me in the ballpark to shag balls.

"Some others – Mickey Cochrane, Goose Goslin and Schoolboy Rowe – can't be here today," Greenberg said at his ceremony, "but I will cherish this moment as long as I live.

"I am proud my name and number will always be remembered for as long as baseball is played in Detroit."

Greenberg not only had to overcome anti-Semitism to excel as a major-leaguer, but his parents expectations as well.

"Growing up in the Bronx with Jewish parents," he said, "naturally they wanted me to be a doctor or lawyer. I decided to be a ballplayer, which immediately characterized me as a bum,

"After that, my parents had three nice kids and a bum."

66 I am proud my name and number will always be remembered for as long as baseball is played in Detroit. 99

July 27, 1997

This is the day Hal Newhouser
– "Prince Hal" - had his No. 16
retired. All his boyhood dreams,
while growing up in Detroit, had
come true.

"This is unbelievable," he said.
"I've completed the whole cycle
and I'm very thankful.

"I waited so long for the Hall of
Fame. That was the ultimate. But
because of the way it all started, I
have a different feeling about my
number. I was a young boy playing
on the sandlots of Detroit, just
wanting to sign with the Tigers."

Newhouser did more than
eventually sign with them. As it
turned out, he achieved greatness
with them.

A dream day for Hal Newhouser.

July 15, 2000

In addition to Willie Horton's No. 23 being retired, a statue of him was unveiled at Comerica Park – during its first year as the Tigers' ballpark.

No stranger to strong emotions, Horton was moved to tears by the honor.

"I think about a promise I made my dad when I signed my first contract (in 1961)," said Willie. "He said I shouldn't sign unless I could make a commitment to the fans. That's the best promise I ever made.

"For every day of my career, I would like to thank the fans for making me part of your family. God bless you."

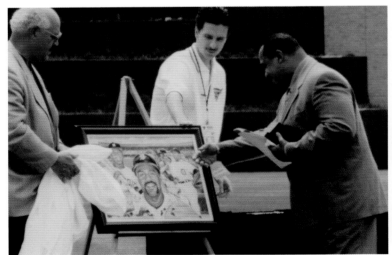

Honoring the great Willie Horton.

> " For every day of my career, I would like to thank the fans for making me part of your family. God bless you. "

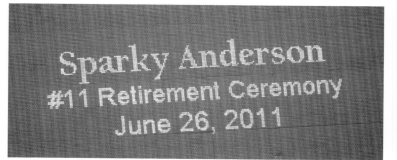

Sparky Anderson
#11 Retirement Ceremony
June 26, 2011

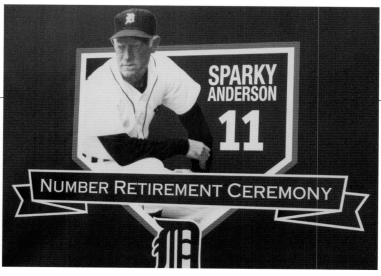

SPARKY ANDERSON
11
NUMBER RETIREMENT CEREMONY

June 26, 2011

The sadness of his day was that the honoree, Sparky Anderson, didn't live long enough to see the Tigers retire his number. He died on Nov. 4, 2010.

But his family was proudly on hand for his number retirement ceremony. And many of the players to whom Sparky had meant so much as the Tigers' manager for 17 years (1979-95) were present as well.

"My father always treated people great," said his daughter Shirlee. "That's just who he was. He loved the people of Detroit."

For Lou Whitaker, who attended the ceremony, the trip to Comerica Park was his first. Trammell also was in town as a coach for the visiting Arizona Diamondbacks.

"Lou's presence just proves the influence Sparky had on so many of us," Trammell said.

Former Tigers' outfielder Larry Herndon was flat-out determined not to miss it.

"Sparky was a life-changer," he said. "I had to be here – because without him, I wouldn't be able to be here."

> " Sparky was a life-changer, I had to be here – because without him, I wouldn't be able to be here. "

– LARRY HERNDON

Sparky's big day.

Pudge, Tram and Jack - all in the Hall.

"You stole a lot of hits from me"- Dave Winfield.

Ten thousand discussions ago.

Two great shortstops – Omar Vizquel and Trammell.

❝ What I'll remember most about him, other than the 1984 World Series and the home runs he hit in it, is the way he played shortstop. As someone who began at that position, and was moved, I marveled at the way he played it. **❞**

– PAUL MOLITOR – ON THE DAY TRAMMELL RETIRED IN 1996. (DETROIT FREE PRESS)

Tigers through and through - Tram, Al and Jim Leyland.

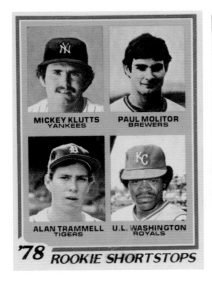

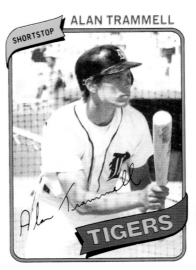

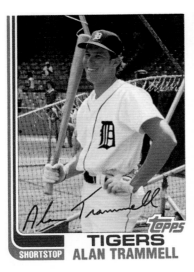

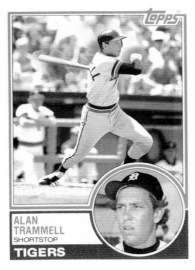

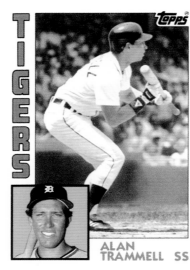

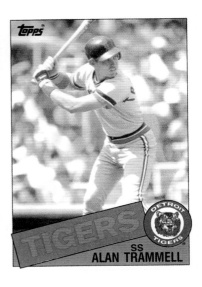

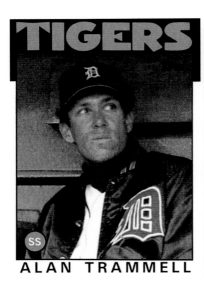

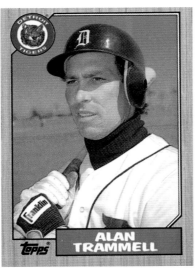

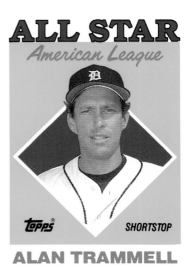

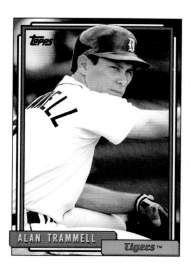

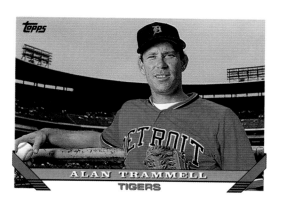

Year	Age	Tm	Lg	G	PA	AB	R	H	2B	3B	HR	RBI	SB	CS	BB	SO	BA	OBP	SLG	OPS	OPS+	TB	GDP	HBP	SH	SF	IBB
1977	19	DET	AL	19	48	43	6	8	0	0	0	0	0	0	4	12	0.19	0.26	0.19	0.44	21	8	1	0	1	0	0
1978	20	DET	AL	139	504	448	49	120	14	6	2	34	3	1	45	56	0.27	0.34	0.34	0.68	89	152	12	2	6	3	0
1979	21	DET	AL	142	520	460	68	127	11	4	6	50	17	14	43	55	0.28	0.34	0.36	0.69	85	164	6	0	12	5	0
1980	22	DET	AL	146	652	560	107	168	21	5	9	65	12	12	69	63	0.3	0.38	0.4	0.78	113	226	10	3	13	7	2
1981	23	DET	AL	105	463	392	52	101	15	3	2	31	10	3	49	31	0.26	0.34	0.33	0.67	92	128	10	3	16	3	2
1982	24	DET	AL	157	556	489	66	126	34	3	9	57	19	8	52	47	0.26	0.33	0.4	0.72	97	193	5	0	9	6	2
1983	25	DET	AL	142	581	505	83	161	31	2	14	66	30	10	57	64	0.32	0.39	0.47	0.86	138	238	7	0	15	4	2
1984	26	DET	AL	139	626	555	85	174	34	5	14	69	19	13	60	63	0.31	0.38	0.47	0.85	136	260	8	3	6	2	2
1985	27	DET	AL	149	678	605	79	156	21	7	13	57	14	5	50	71	0.26	0.31	0.38	0.69	90	230	6	2	11	9	4
1986	28	DET	AL	151	653	574	107	159	33	7	21	75	25	12	59	57	0.28	0.35	0.47	0.82	120	269	7	5	11	4	4
1987	29	DET	AL	151	668	597	109	205	34	3	28	105	21	2	60	47	0.34	0.4	0.55	0.95	155	329	11	3	2	6	8
1988	30	DET	AL	128	523	466	73	145	24	1	15	69	7	4	46	46	0.31	0.37	0.46	0.84	138	216	14	4	0	7	8
1989	31	DET	AL	121	506	449	54	109	20	3	5	43	10	2	45	45	0.24	0.31	0.33	0.65	85	150	9	4	3	5	1
1990	32	DET	AL	146	637	559	71	170	37	1	14	89	12	10	68	55	0.3	0.38	0.45	0.83	130	251	11	1	3	6	7
1991	33	DET	AL	101	421	375	57	93	20	0	9	55	11	2	37	39	0.25	0.32	0.37	0.69	90	140	7	3	5	1	1
1992	34	DET	AL	29	120	102	11	28	7	1	1	11	2	2	15	4	0.28	0.37	0.39	0.76	114	40	6	1	1	1	0
1993	35	DET	AL	112	447	401	72	132	25	3	12	60	12	8	38	38	0.33	0.39	0.5	0.89	138	199	7	2	4	2	2
1994	36	DET	AL	76	311	292	38	78	17	1	8	28	3	0	16	35	0.27	0.31	0.41	0.72	85	121	8	1	2	0	1
1995	37	DET	AL	74	255	223	28	60	12	0	2	23	3	1	27	19	0.27	0.35	0.35	0.7	82	78	8	0	3	2	4
1996	38	DET	AL	66	207	193	16	45	2	0	1	16	6	0	10	27	0.23	0.27	0.26	0.53	34	50	3	0	1	3	0
20 Yrs				2293	9376	8288	1231	2365	412	55	185	1003	236	109	850	874	0.29	0.35	0.42	0.77	110	3442	156	37	124	76	48
162 Game Avg.				162	662	586	87	167	29	4	13	71	17	8	60	62	0.29	0.35	0.42	0.77	110	243	11	3	9	5	3

from baseball-reference.

CONGRATULATIONS, TRAM!

*The Detroit Tigers are proud of your accomplishments
over 20 years wearing the Olde English 'D'.*